Praise for Suicide Survivors Handbook from:

THE BEREAVED:
This book really helped me. It was just as good the second time I read it as it was the first. *Monica N., mother of 15 year-old son died of suicide*

It is the most helpful book I have read on bereavement. It answers the questions we all ask when we're grieving. I think this book is a "must read" for all suicide survivors and their loved ones who feel so incompetent as they search for understanding and ways to help the bereaved. Reading it helped me understand why my precious 13 year-old son died by suicide. *Margaret K., facilitator, Suicide Survivors Support Group, St. Mary's Medical Center*

The chapter on guilt is "right on!" *Mary K, mother whose 15 year-old daughter died of suicide*

THOSE WHO WISH TO HELP THEM:
Educational, touching, and at times painful, no detail is left out. This book comes as the need for it increases. No parent or educator should pass up a chance to read this book.. Trudy provides details from her own experience and valuable secondary sources for a well-rounded and insightful book. *Robin Blatnik, M.A.E.S., English and Composition Instructor*

This is a very well written, thought-provoking, and much needed piece of work. You write with such eloquence about this, I suppose this is why "write what you know" is universally recommended to writers. I was deeply moved by your very absorbing, heartfelt writing. *Patt Jackson, writer, and freelance editor*

Trudy Carlson is a courageous woman. This book, written as a result of her son's suicide, demonstrated the transformative power of grief. It is the first book I would recommend to a survivor of life's worst nightmare--the death of a child by suicide. I learned so much from it. Although Carlson in no way minimizes the extraordinary grief a survivor experiences, she demonstrates how one can grow through adversity, and thus offers hope. *Mara Kirk Hart. Writer, and Teaching Specialist in English and Women's Studies, UMD.*

This is a terrific manuscript. You did a beautiful job of mixing in just the right amount of your personal experience to make the subject real for those who have not directly experienced it. This book is very readable and very practical. I found it helpful and think that many others would too. *Carrie M. Brochardt, M.D., Division of Child and Adolescent Psychiatry, Medical School, University of Minnesota*

Suicide Survivor's Handbook

A Guide to the Bereaved and Those Who Wish to Help Them

Trudy Carlson
Benline Press

PUBLISHER'S NOTE

The ideas, procedures, and suggestions contained in this book are not intended as a substitute for consulting with your physician. All matters regarding your health require medical supervision.

Benline Press, P.O. Box 3032, Mount Royal Station
Duluth, Minnesota 55803

ISBN 096424430-6
Library of Congress No. 94-96837

TABLE OF CONTENTS

ACKNOWLEDGMENT

No book is the product of just one person. My heartfelt gratitude goes to everyone who contributed to it. I want to thank those individuals who read this work in manuscript form at various stages. They include: Roseann Biever, Margaret Kinetz, Monica Natzel, Carol Nord, Caroline Carlson, Garry Carlson, Char Gallian, Mara Kirk Hart, Dr. Kenneth Irons, Ben Wolfe, Lena Biever and Dr. Carrie Borchardt.

I would like to make special mention of Patt Jackson and Robin Blatnik, the editors of the book, whose skill and encouragement helped to make it what it is. Their sustained commitment to this project is the kind of help writers dream of receiving, but never expect to get.

I wish to express appreciation to all the works that are quoted in this book. These works are listed in the bibliography.

There can be no full accounting of the debt I owe the scores of people who contributed to this project by giving me advice and/or technical assistance. They include: Joseph Gallian, James Perlman, Mark Hokkanen, Sheldon T. Aubut, the families of Bill Biever, Allen Biever, Richard Birenbaum, Richard Hartman, Steven Harter, Walter Thill and James Yax.

Finally, my most profound thanks to my fellow members of the Suicide Survivor's Support Group. They were the inspirations for the manuscript as well as the source of most of what I know about this topic.

Introduction

T he death of my son became the birth of this book. Ben was just fourteen years old when he died. You may wonder what could have happened in those few short years to have led him to take his own life. This book will answer that question and others the family and friends of a suicide victim frequently ask. It also answers the questions of those who wish to understand and comfort the survivors, and it gives suggestions on how they can help.

The gifts given to us at the time of Ben's death became the genesis of this book. As memorial money came in, we thought of different ways to use it. My husband Garry and I wanted to do something meaningful with reference to Ben's life as well as our own. A funeral director gave us two suggestions that met these criteria. Half of the memorial money was donated to a program that offers horseback riding experiences for handicapped adults. Ben loved horses, and he also felt close to the residents of the group homes for retarded adults we own and operate. The other half of the money was donated to St. Mary's Grief Support Center in the town where we live, because the funeral director thought we would like to start attending their monthly survivors' meetings.

Ben died on May 31, 1989 and Garry and I attended our first meeting of the survivors group in June. I'll never forget that meeting or my initial reactions to it. As meetings like that generally start, it began with everyone introducing themselves and telling about the events which brought them to the group. I distinctly remember feeling surprised that each person there had lost a close family member through suicide. My reaction was not logical; after all, why else would they have come to the meeting? Logic should have told me each person came there for exactly the same reason I did: to help one another learn to cope with this tragedy. My surprise was based on this question, "how could it be possible that all of those nice people had really experienced a suicide death in their family?"

My attention focused, for obvious reasons, on the parent of another boy who died at age fourteen. During the ninety-minute meeting it became clear his son had been as cherished by him as ours had been by us. After the meeting I asked if my husband and I could meet with him and his wife sometime to talk. His wife invited us to their home for dinner the next week. We discovered one of the things we had in common was a need to turn to books as a source of information in helping to deal with our loss.

As the months went on and we began to either recommend or lend each other books, the idea for a small library developed. Remembering the money Garry and I donated to the Grief Center, I requested it be used to purchase books on suicide and grief for the library. I volunteered to bring the portable library to the meeting each month. After asking advice from the director of the Grief Center about which books to buy, I ordered books and tapes forming the Benjamin Drew Carlson Memorial Library.

Between meetings, the box containing the collection of books is housed in my living room. My interest in the subject and the easy access to the books resulted in my becoming more well-read on the topic than most other bereaved parents. Because of my background as a past university instructor who taught classes in child and adolescent psychology, personality and mental heath, the psychology of the exceptional child, and the psychology of individual differences, I also had a broad foundation from which to understand the nature of the illnesses which cause a death by suicide.

As the librarian of an ever growing collection of books, I attended the support group long after many other parents or close family members usually stopped. This ongoing commitment to the group has been a blessing to me. I never asked: "Do I want to go to the group this month?" The library had to be available to anyone who might benefit from it, and I was the one who brought the box of books! Acting as a librarian, I also came to discover what the members of our survivor group wanted and needed to know.

This handbook combines what I have read, what I experienced as a result of the loss of my own son, and what I have learned from some of the members of the group. The friendships I made there have enriched my life enormously. I will never stop being amazed at the wisdom of the people who sit in our circle as they cope with their tragedies. The experiences they shared have taught me as much as, if not more than, anything I have ever read. What is said during our group meetings is strictly confidential, so none of what appears on these pages came from information shared during the group. Instead, I asked some of members to write about their experience. Their willingness to share what they have learned in their own journey through grief contributed enormously to any wisdom found on these pages.

All of us wish our loved ones had never died. We wish we did not know as much as we do about the grief of a suicide survivor. But since we have this all too intimate knowledge of the subject, we are passing it on to others who may need to know it. The process of doing this is meaningful to us, and we hope it will give you comfort to know you are not alone.

Why?

therapist I respect once taught me never to ask anyone "why" questions because people can't answer them. Conversations based on who, what, where and when are productive, but no one really knows why they did what they did, why they feel the way they do, or why something happened.

This chapter describes the illnesses most often associated with suicide and the symptoms of the various disorders. It will make a distinction between environmental triggers immediately preceding the death, and the suicide victim's long-term struggle with a biological illness. But it can't really answer why the deceased killed themselves, or why they were so unlucky to have their illness in the first place. Only God knows why a person is given a genetic predisposition to a particular illness.

Who are the Victims?

Different authorities will quote different research on suicide statistics, but generally experts agree that of the persons who kill themselves, 30% had pure depression, 30% had depression mixed with alcoholism and/or drug abuse, and 40% had other factors. With a total of 60% of suicides caused by depression in some form, it is the most important illness to understand when trying to learn what underlies such a death. Most people who are depressed also have a problem with anxiety, and alcohol is a drug that acts quickly to reduce the symptoms of anxiety. It is not surprising that many suicide victims use alcohol or drugs to self-medicate their condition.

Although many people with depression also have an anxiety disorder, not everyone who is anxious is also depressed. A sizable percentage of the 40% of persons who commit suicide suffer the panic attacks that can occur in people with anxiety disorder.

Approximately 10% of schizophrenics commit suicide. Schizophrenia is far less common than depression, so although the possibility of suicide is significant for persons with schizophrenia, the total number of suicides with that illness is smaller than those with depression.

Another common reason for suicide involves loss issues. Those who lose their health and suffer from a painful illness may decide to end their life. Someone who experiences a loss of some one or some thing in their life may decide life is no longer worth living.

TYPES OF DEPRESSION

The symptoms of a major (also known as serious or clinical) depression are:

1. *persistent (more than several weeks) sad, anxious or "empty" mood*
2. *feeling of hopelessness or pessimism*
3. *loss of pleasure or interest in ordinary activities, such as sex or spending time with friends*
4. *problems with sleep (insomnia, early-morning waking or oversleeping)*
5. *eating disturbances (loss of appetite or overeating)*
6. *decreased energy; fatigue*
7. *restlessness; irritability*
8. *difficulty concentrating, remembering or making decisions*
9. *inappropriate feelings of guilt*
10. *thoughts of death or suicide ("What is depression").*

With these ten symptoms so clearly set out, it would seem as if anyone could tell when another person is depressed. Certainly a survivor of suicide should have known their loved one was depressed. NOT TRUE! Many people who suffer from this condition do not want their pain to be a burden to others. If their illness does not incapacitate them, they may wear a smile and try to make the best of a bad situation. Many survivors only begin to understand the illness that caused the death of their loved one as they gradually come to see the many subtle ways the illness affected the life of the deceased.

Depression is not just one illness, it is many.

Dysthymia

Dysthymia is chronic low mood which means that people feel out of sorts all of the time. They are not deeply depressed, but neither do they feel good. The weather is a good analogy to use to describe dysthymia. The mood is not like a thunderstorm (dark and dangerous), but the dysthymic doesn't experience blue skies and sunshine either. One could say that the world of the dysthymic is gray and overcast all of the time. They are generally unhappy, but may put on a smile to make other people feel more comfortable. "Researchers estimate that nearly 9 million Americans are locked in dysthymia's dispiriting grip, `It's like a low-grade infection,' says Virginia Commonwealth University clinical psychologist James McCullough. `Dysthymics never really feel good.'" (Goode, 1990).

Ben was dysthymic; his depression was a constant condition throughout his childhood. In fact, Ben told his psychiatrist he felt depressed all of his life. In his medical record she wrote, "He states that he does not remember a time when he has felt happy most of the time."

Dysthymia is not just a minor depressive problem. In a booklet published by the National Institute of Mental Health, we learn that

Some people with dysthymia also have episodes of major depression, their symptoms becoming dramatically more severe for a while and then returning to their usual reduced level. These people are said to have double depression; that is, dysthymia plus major depression. Individuals with double depression are at much higher risk for recurring episodes of major depression, so careful treatment and follow-up are very important. (Sargent, a)

Recurring Unipolar Depression

People with recurring unipolar depressions have depressive episodes with or without some major stressors in their life. These people have normal moods much of the time, but have a number of depressive episodes during their lifetime. When this happens, they have some or many of the ten symptoms described earlier.

Bipolar Illness

Victims of bipolar illness (also known as manic-depressive disorder) enjoy normal moods some of the time, but when they have bouts of this illness, they will alternate between depression and mania. When depressed, they experience many of those ten symptoms listed earlier. When manic they experience:

1. *inappropriate elevation of mood or heightened irritability*
2. *insomnia*
3. *unrealistic notions or self-attitudes*
4. *dramatically increased talking, fidgeting or sexual activity*
5. *racing thought*

6.   *increased risk-taking*
7.   *aggressive response to frustration*
8.   *inability to make decisions*
9.   *inappropriate social behaviors ("What is depression")*

BIPOLAR I

Bipolar illness comes in two forms. People with Bipolar I get very high. They have an unrealistic belief in their own abilities; they may incur horrendous debts and make poor business decisions. They show an increase in talking, as well as physical and social activity. Friends and family see the person as hyperactive. Persons with Bipolar I can have increased sexual activity to the point of being promiscuous. When manic, the person tends to overlook the painful or harmful consequences of any of their behaviors. Their high energy and possible aggressive response to frustration may even result in breaking the law and landing in jail. Lithium, a natural salt, has proven to be effective in stabilizing the highs for persons with this disorder. Physicians have also begun using some of the medications traditionally used to control epilepsy to help people with bipolar illness. The results are promising.

BIPOLAR II

Ben had Bipolar II. His highs did not get extremely high; his manic episodes would have been called hypomanic (small manic). For example, his increased talking was irritating, and I would try to discourage him from dominating or disrupting the family conversations. However, it is unlikely that the casual observer would identify his occasional excessive talkativeness as a problem. His increased physical activity caused him to get too carried away in roughhouse play. For example, Ben loved to wrestle with his dad. When he was younger, his father could just hold him down when Ben got carried away wrestling. But during the last year, there were several times in which Ben, quite unintentionally, hurt his dad during their play. It was our daughter, Caroline, who was more attuned to the problem caused by his slight hyperactivity. She discovered early in her childhood that playing with Ben was often difficult, if not impossible, because he'd get physically out of control. His hypomanic behavior meant that he was not hyper all of the time, but there were times when his behavior was excessive. He did not seem to be able to control this. He never intended to hurt anyone and was always remorseful or confused as to what had come over him.

DEPRESSION IN YOUNG PEOPLE

Until the last few decades, mental health professionals believed that depression in children was impossible. Today's experts know that it exists, and they are attempting to alert family doctors, teachers and counselors. There is no way of knowing if it is as common in children as it is in adults, but there are indications that the percentage for adolescents is similar to that in adults - - 40% (10% severe, plus 30% moderate to mild).

There is not a universally agreed upon list of symptoms of childhood depression. Depression in children and adults is fundamentally the same illness, but it looks different. If we only use the list of adult symptoms, we will miss the symptoms of the vast majority of children suffering from depressive illness.

Lists of symptoms of depression in youngsters have been proposed in the past. Often these lists emphasize changes in the child's behavior, but I do not always find lists that emphasize change to be helpful. For example, children with dysthymia are always feeling somewhat blue. Their depression is not a change in behavior, it is the way they feel every day of their lives. Furthermore, children such as Ben who have bipolar illness have a condition with a very early onset. These children have behaviors, body complaints, frequent illnesses, and mood problems throughout their lives. Their depression is not a change; it is the way they have always been.

Children with recurring unipolar depression on the other hand, do have a normal mood most of the time. A change in mood does signal the onset of a bout with depression for them. I do not want to discount the value of using a change in behavior as useful in diagnosing depression. I just wish to point out that "change" shouldn't be exclusively used as a criteria in defining depression.

This list by Dr. Carl P. Malmquist of the University of Minnesota avoids referring to change. His symptom list includes:

1. *Persistent sadness, in contrast to the temporary unhappy moods that normally occur in all children from time to time.*
2. *Low self-concept.*
3. *Provocative, aggressive behavior, or other behavior that leads people to reject or avoid the child.*
4. *Proneness to be disappointed easily when things do not go exactly as planned.*
5. *Physical complaints such as headaches, stomachaches, sleep problems, or fatigue, similar to those experienced by depressed adults.*

Using Ben as an example where appropriate, I will expand on these five symptoms and then list some which other experts have noted.

1. *Persistent sadness, in contrast to the temporary unhappy moods that normally occur in all children from time to time.*

What are the conditions that might cause persistent sadness? Children with dysthymia will suffer from chronic low mood. Children who suffer from recurring unipolar depression may have the first episode of that condition when they are quite young. Children with bipolar illness have a cyclical condition. Although they will feel normal some of the time, high moods alternate with periods of feeling low. Finally, children who experience a loss of some kind may be beginning a reactive depression that warrants attention. Any child whose sadness persists over a few weeks should be considered for some sort of treatment.

2. *Low Self-concept*

Depressed children typically have problems with self-esteem. It is a mistake to assume their low self-esteem is always a direct result of environmental factors. Even when parents are very loving and careful to avoid criticizing the child, the depressive illness itself can produce an attitude of self-criticism and low self-esteem for the youngster.

Some depressed children have an overly-sensitive disposition which causes them to interpret any general comment as a criticism. This overly sensitive reaction would, also, interfere with their willingness to ask for help in the classroom. The over-sensitivity may also result in the perception that other children are picking on them, when in fact this is not true. Ben perceived lots of bullies in the school yard that probably did not exist; playing with neighborhood children often ended with Ben crying and returning home. His over-sensitivity meant he cried easily and generally had problems getting along with peers. Again, the child's overly-sensitive nature may not have anything to do with the actions of parents who may be doing everything they can to help the child feel confident and secure.

3. Provocative, aggressive behavior, or other behavior that lead people to reject or avoid the child.

Our daughter learned early in her childhood that Ben was difficult to play with. He would provoke disputes between them. Caroline also noted that when he became aggressive, he would either lash out at others or inflict self-injury, such as biting himself. She and her playmates included Ben in their play some of the time, but because they knew that excluding him would mean they could play peacefully, they frequently chose to avoid him.

Ben had marked increases in anger and aggressive behavior when he reached fourth grade. He verbalized his anger, and he broke things like pens and pencils. He also did damage in the house by carving on woodwork and defacing furniture. When Ben began working with his psychiatrist, he mentioned that "his feeling of depression had been worse since about fourth grade." The paradox of the anger expressed by someone with depression is that some of it seems legitimate. Depressed children have every right to feel angry at being misunderstood. They have a right to feel angry at being expected to do things they simply are not able to do. Ben found deep breathing and relaxation methods helpful in controlling his angry feelings.

4. Proneness to be disappointed easily when things do not go exactly as planned.

Ben had a very low tolerance for frustration. When putting together a puzzle, he often pounded on a piece if it did not fit. He did the same to other toys when they did not perform as he wanted. When we would go on a family outing and there was a change or delay in plans, he easily became upset. I have wondered if this proneness to express disappointment is a forerunner to hopelessness and helplessness. Persons with depression often have errors in their thinking which lead them to be more pessimistic than others.

5. Physical complaints such as headaches, stomach aches, sleep problems, or fatigue, similar to those experienced by depressed adults.

Physical pain is a common indicator of childhood depression. People do not generally think of bodily pain in conjunction with depression, but it can be an important symptom. Ben told me about the pains in his arms and legs, but at the time I assumed it was the beginning of childhood arthritis, a condition my husband had when he was a child. I never thought of it as a symptom of depression. Headache pain may be especially important. Ben's childhood was plagued by frequent, painful headaches. Researchers have found that persons who experience frequent migraines have a suicide rate three times higher than people who do not.

Depressed children not only have various aches and pains, but are also frequently ill. This may be due to the effect their depression is having on the immune system. As one person said, "When you are depressed, nothing works well." This includes the immune system. The frequent illness some depressed children have contributes to the aches and pains they experience.

One of the hallmarks of depression is sleep abnormalities. Trouble with sleep can either involve insomnia -- difficulty falling asleep or staying asleep; or the opposite -- sleeping too much. Some children are energized at night and then chronically tired during the day, which adds to their problem with concentration and alertness in school. Ben's difficulties with sleep showed up immediately in infancy, and he did not sleep through the night until he was in his second or third year. Problems with sleep continued throughout his life, and he reported feeling tired at school.

6. *Inability to concentrate*

To Dr. Malmquist's list of symptoms of childhood depression I would add the inability to concentrate. Depressed children have trouble with school. Psychiatrist and author, Dr. Mark Gold writes about the reciprocal connection between depression and school difficulties in a paragraph headed "Learning Disabilities = Depression, Depression = Learning Disabilities. He says,

> Psychologist David Goldstein conducted a five-year study of 159 learning-disabled children in Philadelphia and found that nearly all of them were depressed. The

school problems caused the depression in most of them; but for about one-third, depression produced the school problems.(Gold, 1987)

Scientist have discovered that the limbic system of the brain is of great importance in a person's ability to learn. They also hypothesize that depression is a problem of the limbic system. Little wonder depressed children have learning problems! They may not be able to follow what their teachers say; consequently they do not perform up to their potential.

There are a number of factors that facilitate the vicious circle regarding learning problems and depression. First of all, depressed persons of any age have difficulty concentrating. Add to this a phenomena common in animals as well as in persons called "learned helplessness". Learned helplessness occurs when people or animals find themselves in highly stressful or painful situations which they can neither get out of nor manage to cope with successfully. Children with learning problems are in the classic situation which produces learned helplessness. They are forced to be in a school situation they cannot escape nor cope with successfully. It's easy to see why children with learning problems may begin to feel helpless and hopeless. Ben had both manic-depressive illness and an attention deficit disorder. Either one would have created some problems for him in school; together they served to make it impossible.

7. *Energy fluctuations*

The energy levels of depressed children can fluctuate from normal to hyperactivity and then to sluggishness. Parents find themselves alternating between wanting the child to settle down, and then later wishing the child would do something other than just vegetating in front of the television set. If the child is over-watching TV and not enjoying more active games or hobbies with friends, this may be a clue to some level of depression.

Energy fluctuations are especially true for children with bipolar illness. Pioneer psychiatrist in the treatment of bipolar illness and author, Dr. Ronald Fieve(1975) describes bipolar children this way: "Bursts of aggressiveness and frantic activity may alternate with periods of sluggish passivity in a way that resembles the periodic fluctuations of adult moodswings." It is important to suspect bipolar illness in young children because Dr. Gold(1987) states, "many earlier-onset depressions are now believed to be bipolar II depressions."

8. Eating problems

Another hallmark of depression is eating abnormalities. The child will either eat too little, consequently becoming thin, or eat too much and carry extra weight. Although Ben ate only small quantities of formula as a newborn, he ate frequently and had normal weight. Throughout most of his life Ben struggled with overeating which is consistent with bipolar II. From his work with young patients, Dr. Charles Popper(1990) writes, "appetite and body weight may exhibit marked fluctuations in bipolar children." Dr. Gold(1987) also cites biopolar II as the type of depression with "reverse" symptoms. Patients tend to oversleep rather than have difficulty sleeping and tend to "eat and eat instead of losing their appetites." The connection between eating problems and depressive illness makes me wonder how many overweight children are suffering from an undiagnosed case of depressive illness.

9. Impulsivity

Impulsivity -- acting without thinking about the consequences -- is a major characteristic of children with an attention deficit but is also found in some youngsters with depression. This is especially true of children with bipolar (manic-depressive) illness. Scientific evidence is mounting that bipolar depression is genetically determined. Dr. Gold(1987, p.286) reports, "Many investigators now believe that children who begin a depressed course before puberty are probably genetically driven into such an early expression of the illness." Impulsive children may have either bipolar illness, an attentional deficit, or both. Some experts believe there are many more depressed children with this diagnosis than previously thought.

THE NEED FOR UNDERSTANDING

These following thought-provoking quotes from Dr. Gold act as a conclusion to the information on childhood depression. In them, Gold gives both a perspective on depressive illness and a feeling for how children with the condition are often misunderstood. Gold writes,

Depression in adults and children is remarkably alike...While the symptoms too are similar: sleep and appetite disturbance, bodily complaints, hopelessness, guilt, lack of self-esteem, loss of ability to experience pleasure, fatigue and so on. Children do not express them the same as grown-ups. (1987, pp. 283-284)

If clinicians only use the list of depression in adults when seeking to diagnose children, they will fail to understand most of the cases of depression they encounter in children. There currently is a lack of understanding and treatment of childhood depression. Gold(1987, p.284) states, "Many children end up being treated for hyperactivity and learning disabilities, punished for laziness, or even placed in detention for aggressive, destructive behaviors, when depression is the primary problem."

ANXIETY

Like depression, anxiety is often a biologically based disorder. Symptoms include:

1. *difficulty in getting breath or overbreathing*
2. *skipping or racing of the heart*
3. *sensations of rubbery or "jelly legs"*
4. *bouts of excessive sweating*
5. *smothering or choking sensations or lump in throat*
6. *tingling or numbness in parts of body*

7. *feeling that surroundings are strange, unreal, foggy, or detached*
8. *difficulty falling asleep*
9. *avoiding situations because they frighten you   (Sheehan, 1983)*

Persons with high anxiety may have panic attacks. If these attacks are very severe and frequent, a doctor will diagnose the condition as Panic Disorder.

Panic Attacks

The summer following his sixth grade, I observed what I now know was the first of Ben's panic attacks. We were on a camping trip when Ben reported that his heart was beating fast and he was frightened. He said he could not slow it down and felt like he was having a heart attack. I had Ben lie down and do some deep breathing to help him relax until it passed. I felt badly that a child as young as him should experience something this frightening. Common symptoms during a panic attack include: "sweating, hot or cold flashes, choking or smothering sensations, racing heart, labored breathing, trembling, chest pains, faintness, disorientation or feeling of dying, losing control or losing one's mind"(Mental Health Advocate, 1991). I do not recall exactly how many of these symptoms Ben displayed during the attack, but I do know it was a very painful experience for him to have and for me to watch.

Anxiety and Suicide

The association between anxiety and suicide is multi-faceted. Dr. Jan Fawcett(1992) reports that high anxiety levels and panic attacks may be "distinct short-term predictors of suicide in patients with major depression." Dr. Myra Weissman(1991) has discovered a high risk of suicide in persons with serious anxiety disorders: "20% of patients who experience Panic Disorder at some point in life have made a suicide attempt."

Use of Alcohol and Drugs to Self-Medicate Anxiety

Many of today's parents are frightened their teenager will begin to experiment with drugs and alcohol. What they may not see is often it is the adolescent's attempt to self-treat anxiety and depression. Alcohol is used in these ways:

1.   *It relieves the symptoms of anxiety for those whom anxiety is their only problem.*

2.   *It relieves the symptoms of anxiety for the majority of persons with depression who experience anxiety as a co-morbid condition.*

3.   *It is used by persons with bipolar illness to handle the manic phase of their manic-depressive disorder.*

Without giving a full discussion of the repercussions of excessive drinking, I do wish to emphasize that although alcohol does reduce the symptoms of anxiety, it is itself a depressive drug. It eventually makes the depression worse. If depressed and anxious persons self-medicate with alcohol, they will end up trading reduced anxiety now for greater depression later on. Because alcohol gives them an immediate, though temporary lift, it is hard to convince anxious and depressed people they are actually making the depression worse. Often their solution to lows is to use stimulate drugs to raise their spirits. Other people may see them as being self-destructive, but they may only see they are getting some relief from discomfort.

Anxiety in Childhood

1.   Nail biting

The pictures I have of Ben are a blessing to me because they bring to mind things I might have otherwise forgotten. When Ben was approximately eighteen months old, my husband Garry took a series of pictures of him, his sister, and me. In one of them, Ben was chewing on his nails. Ben always did that. The picture reminds me how young he was when anxiety showed itself to be an integral part of his experience throughout life.

2.   *Bladder and bowel problems*

Bedwetting is mentioned by many psychiatrists in relationship to both anxiety and depression. Ben was toilet trained at two-and-a-half, but bedwetting started at age five. Nothing we tried was successful in treating this problem. Not every child who has a bedwetting problem is anxious and depressed, but if a parent or doctor sees a cluster of symptoms indicative of either of these conditions in addition to the bedwetting, it is possible that the wetting is yet another symptom.

3.   *Excessive fearfulness*

Anxiety is defined as fearfulness in situations that do not pose any realistic danger. The world is a scary place for anxious children, filled with danger and menace. It is puzzling to parents to see excessive fearfulness in their child when they are providing the youngster with a safe and secure environment. This certainly was the case with our family. I thought it would be possible to teach Ben to be unafraid by being calm myself and by giving him information that demonstrated the safety of the situation. Although those strategies are generally advisable and I had some success, I was unable to calm his fears completely.

SCHIZOPHRENIA AND SUICIDE

Schizophrenia is a serious and chronic brain disease of unknown origin which affects 1% of the population. It typically starts in adolescence or during young adulthood. The symptoms are:

1. *delusions*
2. *hallucinations*
3. *thinking disturbances*
4. *volitional changes.*

Dr. Alec Roy(1992), Associate Professor of Psychiatry at the Albert Einstein College of Medicine, reports that, "Suicide has long been recognized as a hazard of this illness. Studies now show that up to 10% of schizophrenics die by committing suicide. The first few years of schizophrenic illness are the period of greatest risk." Schizophrenics who commit suicide tend to be male and young. Since 1980, twelve studies reported finding that 70% of schizophrenic suicides were male and their mean age was 34 years. While 30% committed suicide while they were hospitalized, Roy reports that the first few weeks and months after discharge from hospital are the period of greatest suicide risk.

The presence of depression along with the schizophrenia increases the risk for these patients. Dr. Roy(1992) indicates that "altered moods were present in 60% of those who commit suicide."

CO-MORBIDITY AS A FACTOR IN SUICIDE

From what has been written here about depression, anxiety and schizophrenia, it becomes apparent that co-morbidity (having two problems rather than one) puts people in especially high risk for suicide. If one is depressed, the addition of anxiety will increase the likelihood of suicide. If one is anxious and use alcohol or drugs to self-medicate, these substances will increase depressive moods and put a person at higher risk for suicide. And if one is schizophrenic, experiencing a bout of depression will increase the likelihood of suicide. You will recall that persons with only one problem -- pure depression -- account for 30% of the suicide rate. Serious depression by itself causes many deaths. When people have more than just one condition to cope with, the risk of suicide rises. It is not difficult to understand how they come to feel overwhelmed.

ILLNESSES ORIGINATING IN OTHER PARTS OF THE BODY

Little is written about those people who kill themselves because they have an incurable or fatal disease. Perhaps because their illness is obvious to everyone, there is little need to explain to the survivors about the pain the suicide victim was suffering. When a person has a fatal disease, the survivor is less likely to be plagued by the question, "Why did he kill himself?" It is also easier to understand the hopelessness the suicide victim may have felt.

OTHER CAUSES

Some previously undepressed people temporarily become victims of a depression as a reaction to an incident in their lives. Often it is a loss of health, of a loved one, of a job, or of money. The stories of suicides in the early days of the Great Depression after the stock market crash of 1929 are famous. We also have read of people who kill themselves soon after the loss of a loved one.

Depression caused by environmental factors is called reactive depression because it is a reaction to an event or condition in life. This depression can be very severe, but many people recover without experiencing a recurrence.

ENVIRONMENTAL TRIGGER VERSUS A STRUGGLE WITH LONG-TERM ILLNESS

In past decades there has been an overemphasis on the environmental stressors which immediately precede a suicide. There has also been an emphasis on looking for warning signs.

Neither of these strategies has been particularly helpful. The environmental stressors are the every day stresses that all of us face. My son died at the end of the school year when incomplete work could no longer be put off. This and my conversation with him regarding his overeating were probably the triggers for his suicide. Overemphasis on triggers (environmental factors immediately preceding the death) not only prevents us from having a clear understanding of the cause of the problem -- the psychiatric illness -- but when we over-emphasize the preceding stressor, it may encourage the survivors to torture themselves unnecessarily. After a suicide, survivors often say, "If only I had done this or if I had done that the suicide may have been prevented." The truth is that the person's suicide may have had little, if anything, to do with the person's actual life situation.

> Recent work comparing the lives of those who kill themselves, those who attempted, and those who died of natural cause¾reveals that, in the main, the lives of those who kill themselves are often no worse than those of others who carry on. To the objective outsider, their situations are far from hopeless, and there are ways other than suicide to solve their problems.("Useful information on suicide")

It is not so much the circumstances of a person's life, but the pain of their illness which is relevant.

Looking for warning signs is equally unhelpful in preventing suicide. Many of the suicide survivors who come to our group report that there were little, if any, of the signs so frequently cited in the literature on suicide. An emphasis on looking for warning signs only makes the survivor feel neglectful by encouraging a false assumption that if only they would have been alert the person would not have died.

Scientists are trying to find the symptoms most indicative of an imminent risk for an attempt to commit suicide. Factors such as high anxiety, panic attacks, a marked decrease in the ability to concentrate, loss of the ability to experience pleasure, and insomnia are emerging as important indicators of high risk. More research is still needed, and it takes time to re-educate the general public about the actual factors that could alert them to danger.

WHY DOES SOMEONE COMMIT SUICIDE?

Why did my son die? I can't answer that, but I also can't answer the question "Why was he born?" It is relevant to ask, "Why is anyone born?" Like most everyone else, I studied biology and learned about sperm and ova. But the miracle behind conception and birth remains a mystery. Ben's death by suicide is a mystery, but is not everyone's death a mystery? Why does someone get cancer? Like most other people, did not my son die as a result of his illness?

What About Shame & Guilt?

W hen I was developing the outline for this book, my husband Garry said "You have to write a chapter about guilt." It might surprise you that I feel little, if any, guilt concerning Ben's death. Because of this, I wondered how I could write convincingly about guilt. One night I slept on this question, and awoke the next morning with an answer. What I needed to communicate is the reason why no one else needs to feel guilty, either.

The premise of this chapter is that a certain amount of guilt is natural, perhaps even unavoidable, especially for parents. The role of a parents is to care for and protect their child. This role is universal throughout most creatures on this planet, whether it is an animal such as a bird or a mammal or a human being. With our human consciousness we will have some level of guilt for failure to succeed in the role of protector and care giver. We will likely feel something we did, or failed to do, caused or contributed to the death.

It is not only family members who may feel guilty. Everyone who knew the person well may tell themselves "if only I had done such and such, the person might not have died." Keeping this in mind, the second premise of this chapter is that the most effective weapon against excessive or unnecessary guilt is logic. In dealing with the topic of guilt, I want to define it more clearly, and make a distinction between it and shame. Authors typically write not only about the guilt many survivors experience, but also their shame. Both factors are important.

SHAME

Shame is the emotion felt when one does not meet the expectation of others. Shame is the concern expressed when you ask the question, "What will other people think of me?" In the case of a suicide the concern is, "Will other people assume I am a bad person or there was something wrong with my family because one of its members took his or her life?"

I was extremely lucky in never feeling any shame in connection with Ben's death. If you were to ask me why this is true, I can only guess that perhaps it had something to do with my background as a child and as an adult. In many respects I have been lucky. I am the youngest of nine children, and throughout childhood I was aware of being one of my mother's favorites. Although my parents made every effort to treat all of their children equally, I think it is fair to say I was indulged more than my other brothers or sisters. For example, being the baby in the family meant there was no need to relinquish my spot on my mother's lap to a younger sibling.

I was also the little girl who was still at home each day at the time of my older sister's death. I was just four years old when she died. Being with my mother as she was going through her own grief process may have contributed to my becoming especially important to her. Whatever the reason for my mother's favoritism towards me, I grew up with the feeling of total acceptance. Shame is not an emotion I expect to feel.

My parents were well liked in the close knit rural community of my childhood. Consequently, nothing in my formative years even vaguely resembling shame was associated with my family. Even though I no longer live in that particular community, my expectation of how others will treat me has not changed. Feeling shame in connection with the death of my child would have been foreign to my way of thinking.

GUILT

Guilt is the emotion associated with the failure to meet the expectations you set for yourself. It is the emotion felt when you think you have not done something you personally feel you should have done. Again I look to my background to explain my relative lack of guilt. My mother and father were strict but fair and loving. They were not perfect, but they were "good enough parents" - all that is necessary to raise healthy children who grow up to become responsible adults. I had no particular reason to doubt that I too would be a "good enough parent" to a healthy child. My studies as a psychology major, my experience as an elementary teacher, and my work as a university instructor gave me a background helpful to being a "good enough parent."

I was <u>not</u>, however, given a healthy child. Ben's complex depressive illness, his anxiety disorder, and his attention deficit disorder were a triple disability for him and an enormous challenge for me. Ben and I did everything we could think of to cope with his many problems. I helped him at home and tried to get help for him through the school system. When that failed, we hired a private tutor. He went through a three-day assessment at the Mayo Clinic to accurately diagnose his problem. He was receiving treatment, including medications, through university hospitals. At home we used many self-help strategies including behavior modification, cognitive therapy, relaxation techniques, visualization, and self-esteem enhancement programs.

Many of you reading this list may paradoxically begin to feel guilty because you did not do all or some of these things. To this I would reply.

1) My background and interest in psychology would, of course, make me familiar with therapeutics appropriate for his emotional problems. A typical parent would not be expected to have this level of familiarity.

2) As the owner and operator of small group homes for developmentally disabled adults (mini-medical facilities), I took clients to doctors frequently and became comfortable dealing with a wide variety of medical conditions as well as with the use of medications.

Of course I would be more comfortable going to the Mayo Clinic, going to a university hospital, and using psychotropic medications than would the typical parent. My relatively unusual background put me in a position to pursue many strategies to help a child with a mood disorder. I did more than most parents might have, but EVERYONE does the best they can and SO DID YOU. Remember, I did all that for my son, but he still committed suicide.

After Ben's death, I went through the list of all the things we had done over the years. Still plagued by the question, "Was not there something more we could have done to help him?", I came up with one thing we could have been done which we hadn't tried—group therapy! I had not gotten Ben into a support group for depressed persons.

He did participate in a group at school that dealt with the dangers of alcohol and drugs. He even went on to join a special group for junior high youngsters who may be at risk for having problems. But since I had not encouraged him to join the adult manic-depressive support group in our city, I felt I could accuse myself of failing to get him ALL of the help I possibly could have gotten for him.

Talking to my mother about this on the phone one day, she firmly responded with, "Just cut it out!" I wish I could somehow impart to you these same words with the authority my mother had with me. If I knew you were torturing yourself, I would say "JUST CUT IT OUT!"

IF ONLY...

No matter what the cause of death, people play the "if only" tape over and over in their heads. When the death is a suicide, you will certainly play that tape as much, if not more, than anyone else. When I play that tape I can say, "If only I would not have left him alone that night, he might not have killed himself." The truth is he might not have died on May 31, 1989. But what about June 1, 2, 3? What about July, August, September? What about 1990, 1991 and 1992? When a youngster is at high risk and his desire to kill himself comes often, you will prevent his death several times, even many times, but ultimately your luck may run out. If his illness is not as severe and the wish to die does not inflict itself as frequently, family and friends may be able to prevent it as often as it occurs. No one can know for sure which suicides are preventable and which ones are not.

Looking back, I know we prevented Ben from hurting himself several times. We were not aware then that he was suicidal, but we did see him through times when he was extremely upset. Perhaps Ben's psychiatrist's words, "He had many high risk behaviors and your getting him through as far as he came is a credit to the care you gave him," applies as much to you as it does to us.

Treatment for depression is successful for at least 80% of the people who have the condition. With a success rate that high, of course people with depression should seek help. Everything should be done to publicize the good news that four out of every five people who suffer the pain of depression can look forward to an end to their pain! Those of us who have lost someone we love dearly to suicide do not deserve to torture ourselves with the assumption that "if only they had gotten treatment they would be alive today." That statement may be true for some suicide victims, but there is no evidence it is true for a majority of them. Approximately 15% of people with depression kill themselves. I ask, is there any evidence that some of these are not among the nearly 20% of persons who are not successfully treated by current anti-depressant medications?

If someone has cancer, their chance of surviving depends to an extent on what kind of cancer it is, how long they have had it, and where the cancer is located. Some kinds of cancers have a good prognosis. Others do not. When my father-in-law had a throat cancer, his doctor told him he had an excellent chance for total recovery. Years later when his wife was diagnosed with cancer of the pancreas, his first reaction was, "I had cancer and recovered. She can to." Nothing was further from the truth.

The vast majority of depressions have an excellent prognosis, but some depressions are either frequently reoccurring or subside but never totally go away. We do a disservice to ourselves, and dishonor the memory of the suicide victim, if we minimize the seriousness of the individual's particular illness.

My thirteen year old sister died of a rheumatic heart condition. My parents preserved her life for many years by strictly enforcing this rule: Ellen must not run. But then came the day when she found herself without the watchful eye of someone in authority. She ran on the playground and died. My parents prevented her death for a long time, but like me, one day their luck ran out and their child died.

The parents of young suicide victims are especially vulnerable to guilt because parents are told they are responsible for their child's behavior. That expectation is not even logical! Parents of any species need to care for their offspring. Supervising them is part of protecting them—the second part of the instinctive role of a parent. Care and supervision is, however,

something very different from being responsible for someone
else's behavior. No one is ever responsible for what another
person does.

        If the suicide victim is your child, your spouse, your
significant other, your sibling, or your friend, their behavior was
their decision. They may have come to the decision to die as a
result of the distorted thinking which characterizes their illness.
The pain of their illness undoubtedly contributed as well to the
suicide. In many respects one could say their death was not their
fault. What can be said with certainty is that their suicide was not
your fault.

How long does the pain last?

Whenever the newly-bereaved join our grief support group, bringing with them fresh, raw pain, I always hesitate to tell them the truth about how long their pain will last. I am equally shy about letting them know that things are likely to get worse before they get better. It seems inconceivable that anything could be worse than what they have just been through. But for some of us, the months after the death are worse than the first weeks immediately following the suicide.

My intention is not to over-generalize what I write about the grief process; everyone's grief is different. I can only share what some research has found is often true; what I have personally experienced, and what other people in my support group went through. Everyone's journey will be unique. There is no correct way to get through this, no right amount of time it should take, and no moment in which things will be totally healed.

In many respects, a suicide is like any other unexpected death. Robbed of time before the death to become prepared for it, the bereavement necessarily takes a long time. For most of us, the painful grief will last for several years although, due to the cyclical nature of the process, the pain will vary dramatically from day to day, week to week and month to month.

STAGES

Dr. Robert Veninga's recent book on loss, The Gift of Hope, gives one of the finest descriptions of a typical pattern people go through when tragedy strikes. After the loss of a close friend, Veninga asked 115 people with a variety of serious losses to describe their experiences. From his research, he discovered five common stages.

STAGE ONE: THE BOMB SHELL

The person's first reaction to the tragedy is to become numb, emotionless. In this dazed state, one survivor may sit motionless in a chair or even go to sleep while another may reach out to others. This stage usually lasts only a day or a day and a half. Veninga found during this stage the survivor usually:

1.   *Is unable to make decisions.*

Because they are overwhelmed by the loss, people have little ability to think objectively or analytically. The survivors have difficulty concentrating.

2.   *Has trouble carrying on a conversation with family or friends.*

Bereaved people may stop in the middle of what they were saying, not knowing what they had been talking about. The nature of what is said may range from profound sadness one moment to almost euphoria the next.

3.   *Experiences anxiety.*

Veninga reports that survivors' reactions to anxiety range from hyperactivity and excessive talking in some people to a desire to withdraw in others. Still other survivors will experience bodily reactions such as stomach upset or nausea.

Dr. Veninga's research lead him to conclude that the best thing to do for persons when the bombshell hits is to let them know you are available to help in any way the survivor feels is appropriate. Bereaved persons may not want advice or even your presence during that time. But knowing you care and are willing to do whatever would be helpful is greatly appreciated during the first few days.

STAGE TWO: DELIBERATE ACTIVITY

Veninga quotes Lady Bird Johnson, "Grief carries its own anesthesia," to describe why it is that survivors are often able to function competently during the funeral and in the weeks that follow. This anesthesia allows the person to make the necessary funeral arrangements and write all the thank you notes. Propelled by a strong need to put their lives in order, some survivors can work with energy and efficiency for those weeks, while at the same time they experience decreased appetite, problems concentrating, difficulty sleeping, and fatigue. Even with the presence of these symptoms, family and friends marvel at how well the survivor is coping with the loss. Determined to carry on, the person works hard to survive.

STAGE THREE: "HITTING ROCK BOTTOM"

With the numbness of stage one gone, and the anesthesia of stage two worn off, stage three is the most painful part of grief. Although everyone is different, people who experience a serious loss often reach stage three around four months after the loss. Anger is the hallmark of this period. Something precious has been stolen from the person's life. Anger is the natural reaction to any loss. The anger which rages during this time is like a storm. Veninga says this storm sometimes erupts into a burning resentment, while at other times it simmers quietly. Like any other storm, the anger of grief ultimately wears itself out. In its place comes a new, quieter, more poignant emotion: loneliness. It is the awareness that in our voyage through life, we are ultimately alone. We may have a spouse, parents, children, siblings and devoted friends, but despite their love and support, each of us is still alone. No one can take our pain away. We have to go through this by ourselves.

Veninga discovered that in stage three, persons who experience tragic loss become fearful, and their thinking is characterized by four negative themes:

1.   *My life will never be the same.*

When tragedy strikes, the person feels less secure about life in general, and less optimistic about the future. Before the knowledge of how cruel life can be is made manifest, the individual may have had the belief that life is simple and good. After life strikes its blow, optimism temporarily gives way to excessive pessimism.

2.   *I have let everybody down.*

In an early attempt to answer why the tragedy happened, the survivors logically assume they are responsible for it. They feel guilty of some sin of commission or omission which they feel brought on this tragedy.

3.   *I will never be happy again.*

A sense of hopelessness about the future will temporarily exist to some extent in most survivors of tragedy. The more options survivors can identify and develop into viable opportunities, the less hopeless they will feel. They need not act on these options immediately, but they need to perceive them as possibility in the future.

4.   *My spouse doesn't understand me.*

Marriage is often one of the casualties of loss. There is a common misconception that tragedy pulls people together, when in fact it puts a strain on the family. If the marriage was strong before the tragedy, it usually can withstand the severe strain brought about by loss. If the marriage was already weak, it may not survive.

Variations in the way each spouse grieves is a primary stressor on the marriage. For example, I was very work-oriented after the death of our son Ben. My husband spent more time thinking about the loss. These two very different coping mechanisms can add to the feeling of not being understood. Couples who have been married a long time often come to accept and even respect each other's coping mechanisms even when they are very different from their own.

Not only are there variations in patterns but in the amount of time it can take to go through the stages. One spouse may go through a particularly painful period, while the other is spared. All of this can create further tension in the marriage or increase the feeling of being misunderstood by the spouse.

There are, however, marriages in which the voyage through tragedy creates a bond. My husband and I may not have always liked each other during the years following Ben's death, but we are still together. Ours is one of those long-term marriages that was able to withstand tragedy.

VENINGA CALLED STAGE FOUR: THE
AWAKENING

Hope is the word which characterizes this period. The fear that dominated the previous stage gradually gives way to the beginning of guarded optimism. This is especially true if the person can develop a personal meaning for the tragedy. Veninga and I share a high regard for the work and writings of psychiatrist and concentration camp survivor, Dr. Viktor Frankl. I summarize his philosophy later in the book, but for now will just say that hope is based on the belief that our tragedies are not meaningless accidents. Something of lasting value can arise from the most painful of losses.

STAGE FIVE: ACCEPTANCE

The acceptance of loss is based on two concepts found in the philosophy of India:

1.   Duragraha

Duragraha is a type of stubbornness in which the person is able to become objective about suffering. It is a decision to not allow the tragedy to destroy you.

2.   Satyagraha

Satyagraha is a willingness to take advantage of what life does have to offer. It is the ability to bring joy back into life by consciously appreciating what you have. It is gratitude for the love of those closest to you as well as opening up with warmth to new people who enter your life. Satyagraha is the wisdom that all life is a mixture of suffering and joy.

MY PATTERN

I find it hard to put a label on the first seven days after Ben's death. To say it was excruciating implies it was one-dimensional. It would negate the sense of alertness I had to the fact that this single event was the most important event of my life. I sensed a need to pay attention, not only to the tragedy of Ben's death, but also to the power and mystery involved. If I were to use a single phrase to describe the emotional paradox experienced in the first week, it would be—it was a rich experience. It was filled with great appreciation for family and friends, profound sadness, and a sense of mystery concerning the meaning of life.

My energy was high the first week. Ben died on a Wednesday night. The funeral was the following Monday: on Tuesday my sister-in-law helped me organize the thank you notes, which I completed on Wednesday and mailed on Thursday morning. I have never been more efficient before or since!

In the nine weeks which followed, it was my belief that Ben's distorted thinking had led him to feel that everyone would be better off if he were dead. His pain would end and we would no longer have to deal with his condition or provide him with help. He had found a way to take care of his illness and disability himself. He had come up with a permanent solution to his difficulties. His death, of course, was not something anyone really wanted, but if his distorted thinking led him to believe that his death was in some way a gift to us, I did not want to reject it. If Ben had intended me to go on with my life without him, then I wanted to honor his wishes by living as fully and as joyfully as I could.

The pattern I found myself in between June 6 and August 13 was a three day cycle: two days of high energy and good mood, followed by one day of feeling totally devastated. This ongoing three day cycle meant that I was able to work efficiently for two days, while barely functioning on the third. I would feel almost joyful as I kept very busy, filling every moment with work on the first days, while closing the doors of my office to give myself privacy as I grieved on the third.

August 12 is my daughter's birthday, and I managed to celebrate it in some sort of cheerful fashion. It acts as a landmark in my mind, the last of the good days I would have for many months to come. From August 13 to approximately December 31, I do not remember having any good days. There was no more temporary joy, no energy, little ability to concentrate on anything but the loss of my son. It was then I began writing about his life and his death. I used writing as therapy. Desperately wanting to clarify for myself that we had done everything we could to help him, I found it helpful to recall and record everything we had tried in an attempt to help him in coping with his problems. (The therapeutic effects of writing during the grief process are more fully explored in the next chapter.) I also read extensively during those months.

The dark cloud which hung over me for four and-a-half months lifted around January 1. The change was so dramatic it caused me to conclude that my grief was over. I remember thinking I must have done such a great job of thoroughly grieving I got all my grief work done during one intensely painful period. This unexpected high mood lasted for just a week or two until I caught the flu. Sick and tired, I once again felt low. After recovering from this brief illness, I found myself in a new cyclical pattern. I could function fairly well during most of the day, if I cried for 15 - 20 minutes each day. During the rest of the day my mood was neither joyful nor low. Although I could concentrate on my work, at the same time Ben's death was never really out of my mind. From January 1 - July 15 I also had occasional periods (approximately one week in length) every month to six weeks in which my mood and energy were low. After July 15 the need to cry daily gradually decreased but I still had occasional crying spells. The week-long periods of low energy and mood gradually became less numerous and less serious.

What is it like for me five years later?

I can write easily about Ben's death, but if I were to talk to someone who did not know about the death of my child, I would be unable to do so without showing emotion. I have not had any weeks as painful as those I experienced during the first year, but I still have hard days. Because of the cyclical nature of grief, I can not be totally sure I will not ever have long periods of pain. If confronted with a new death of a loved one, I do not honestly know how I would respond. It is very possible it would throw me once again into the same kind of grief I had during the first year. My intuition tells me, however, the pain would not last as long as it did then.

None of us will ever be quite the same. Our lives have changed forever, but we can use our suffering to lend sympathy and support to others who may benefit from our understanding.

What helps?

F ive months after Ben's suicide, my husband and I went
to a weekend conference for bereaved parents. The
keynote speaker was a funeral director with
extraordinary insight into the needs of the bereaved. He
said there are two things parents who lose a child need:
objective information and emotional support.

Nothing in my experience over the past five years
conflicts with his assertion. I found myself craving information. I
first turned to Ben's psychiatrist. Ben's routine three-week
appointment had been scheduled for the Friday after his funeral.
I asked his psychiatrist if it would be possible for my husband
and me to keep the appointment. I told her I believe there is
strength in truth. I wanted to know what I could about Ben's
condition.

I had the impression she genuinely wanted us to come to
talk with her and was just as interested in talking with us as we
were in meeting with her. At the session, she listened carefully to

us. Our meeting was more a therapy session than an exchange of new information. We clarified our feelings and hopefully avoided some distortions in our own thinking. We came to grips with the actual seriousness of the medical condition that caused Ben's death. The session met our needs for emotional support and objective information.

EMOTIONAL SUPPORT

After a suicide, you will need all the friends you can get. Support can come from sources you expect, such as members of your church, but this might not be your experience. A disappointing response from church may not be related to the actual cause of the death. People who have lost a loved one expectedly after a long illness such as cancer, or unexpectedly from an accident or heart attack, may also have a disappointing lack of support from church. Strong support for the bereaved probably exists in those churches in which either the minister or a small group in the congregation take a special interest in supporting the bereaved and make it a priority in their church community.

As a suicide survivor, friends who are willing to listen to you talk are your main source of support. Since the majority of your grief work begins after three or four months, friends who are only willing to talk with you right after the incident will not be of much help. People who have had some serious loss themselves or some major disappointment in their own lives are usually sensitive to your loss. Those friends may not be able to completely understand what you are going through, (no one can;

each situation is unique) but they can relate to your pain in their own way, listen to your story, and share their own.

Our suicide survivors' support group meets once a month. In the first year following Ben's death, I did not think a once-a-month meeting was frequent enough to meet our needs. I talked with the director of the Grief Center and he informed me we were welcome to join one or more of their other groups in addition to the suicide group. There is a group for parents who lost a child (school age or older) from any cause, and a general group for anyone who lost a loved one.

My husband and I began attending the other parents' group. It was helpful not only because of the added emotional support we received but because it gave us a more balanced perspective on Ben's death. We found we had a lot in common with the other parents who had lost a child, especially if the loss was unexpected. When a loved one dies from a car, motorcycle or recreational vehicle accident, the survivors are tortured with "why," "if only," and with guilt and anger similar to (although not exactly like) that of a suicide survivor.

A sudden death caused by the person's biology can even have this impact on the survivor. In the past few years, Garry and I had the opportunity to meet three sets of parents whose healthy adolescents died when the young person's heart just stopped beating. It is similar to Sudden Infant Death Syndrome, but happens to a child who is older—in the three cases it was a young person between the ages of fourteen and twenty. Meeting these parents taught Garry and me that a death by suicide does not necessarily create a unique grief experience. <u>We are much</u>

more like others than we are different. A death of a child is a death of a child, no matter what the cause.

A specific suicide support group is helpful, however, because the bereaved has a desire to find others whose situation is as close to their own as possible. This certainly was true for me. It meant a lot to Garry and I to meet the father of another fourteen year old at our first suicide survivors meeting. We felt a strong need to talk with him. We discovered we had much in common—he and his wife teach at a university; my husband and I are both former university instructors. The similarities between our situations made me feel that I was not alone. We were lucky to have a suicide support group in our city. If there is one in yours, I highly recommend you at least try it. You owe it to yourself to meet some of the wonderful and wise people who attend those sessions.

A group setting is helpful because of the friendships made there and because members share a variety of experiences. But some people are uncomfortable in groups. Individual counseling by someone at a grief center, a minister at church, or a psychologist at his office can be helpful to persons who prefer a private conversation to a group meeting. The credentials of the person doing the counseling are not as important as the comfort level you have with the person. I remember the comment Ben's psychiatrist once made to him. "No one can help you if you don't like them."

Realizing that after the death of a loved one you will need all the help you can get, many survivors find it helpful to seek both private counseling and attend support groups. Some do one first and then the other, while many survivors do both at the same time, especially during the third stage of grief when the numbness and anesthesia have worn off, and they are left to face the full pain of the loss.

READING

No matter what the cause of death, (whether it is a prolonged and painful illness in the body or in mind) most survivors hunger to learn as much as possible about the illness underlying the death. Suicide survivors ask "why," whether or not they were aware of the existence of depression and/or anxiety. I was aware of my son's illnesses and was reasonably well informed about them before his death. But after Ben died, I read everything I could about these disorders, especially in children.

Books are available any time, night or day, whenever you need them, whereas, people aren't. It is possible to read twelve hours a day when you are having a rough time. Even the most supportive friend isn't usually available for that length of time. Another great thing about books is that they are an important source of objective information, one of the two basics necessary for recovery.

Inspirational books can be just as much help as scientific ones. Similarly, books on the grief process itself may be just what you need at some point. Let your intuition be your guide in telling you what you need at any given moment. At the back of this book is a bibliography you may find helpful.

WRITING

Writing helped me so much and in so many ways that my list of benefits may not fully cover what I received from it.

1.   Like reading, writing is available when people aren't.

If I choose, I can write from 9 p.m. to 3 a.m. How many friends are willing to talk to you during those hours?

2.   Like reading, writing is possible for extended periods of time.

You can choose to write twelve hours a day, two or three days in a row. No friend can avoid burnout listening to you for that length of time, even if you do hold your conversations during reasonable hours of the day.

3.   Writing doesn't necessarily interfere with your job.

You can do it early in the morning, late at night, or on weekends. It offers complete flexibility; you can even do it while you are sitting in a waiting room, thereby taking advantage of what would otherwise be a waste of time.

4.   Writing is affordable.

Pencils and paper are relatively cheap. No one but the very wealthy could afford to pay the counseling bill for the same level of acceptance and therapy that is received from an inexpensive pad of paper.

5.   *Writing allows you to express your anger without hurting others.*

You can get as angry as you need to get and express it as strongly as you like without doing any damage to the people you love or to friends who may be innocent bystanders. I was angry for a long time, and writing proved to be a reliable method of helping me throughout it.

6.   *Writing helps you to be logical and objective.*

Perhaps one of the reasons for my relative lack of guilt regarding Ben's death was the list I created which outlined

- a. his symptoms throughout his life
- b. the nature of his three separate conditions: the depressive illness, the   anxiety disorder, and the ADHD (Attention Deficit Hyperactivity   Disorder)
- c. the attempts we made to obtain help for him through the school system
- d. the private tutoring we paid for
- e. the variety of other things that we did to help him cope
- f. the medical evaluations
- g. the medication and therapy that were in place at the time of his death

Your list may not be exactly like mine, but the survivors I have met are equally blameless, and they would be helped by making an objective list of all they did to care for their loved ones.

7.   *Writing allows you to describe exactly what your feelings are regarding the death.*

As I worked through my anger, I discovered what I really was angry at. It wasn't at Ben, or at myself, or at anyone else. I was not even angry at God. I was just angry that life turned out to be this hard. The one phrase that best described my emotion was: profound disappointment. I discovered this through writing.

Different Types of Writing

Most people's grief writing consists of keeping a journal where they can write anything. They can express their anger, their guilt, or answer all of their "why" questions in the journal. Writing poetry, or copying a poem they find meaningful to them, is also comforting Writing letters to the person who has died can be helpful, especially if the survivor suffers from regrets over things not said to the suicide victim when he or she was alive. Writing to the deceased allows you to say what you want to express or to say good-bye. Letters can also express the love you have for the deceased, the anger you feel because of the death, or your forgiveness to the person for the pain it has caused. What do you most need to express? What are your burning questions? Consider putting them in a letter. You may be surprised at the information that comes out of your pencil in reaction to any questions you put on paper.

If writing is done with future publication in mind, it will force you to review what you have written and revise it over and over and over again. This demands that you be as objective, as precise, and as accurate as you possibly can, all of which forces you to be logical. By forcing you to clarify things in your own mind, writing is cognitively therapeutic as well as emotionally healing.

PAYING ATTENTION TO
YOUR PHYSICAL HEALTH

Grief is hard on every aspect of your health. All the recommendations coming out of the wellness movement in the past twenty years apply to people in grief. I do not need to repeat everything you have heard about the value of proper nutrition and sensible exercise here, except to say that many bereaved people find regular outdoor walks especially helpful. Perhaps it is the combination of the exercise, being in nature, and talking with a close friend that produces the benefit. Whatever the reason or reasons, long walks are helpful during grief.

DO SOMETHING YOU ENJOY

Taking time to do something you enjoy sounds like one of those pieces of well meaning advice that at first glance seems light, airy, and simplistic. You are facing the darkest, heaviest, and most complex thing in your life. How can you possibly take this suggestion seriously? Enjoyment and appreciation, when viewed as spiritual discipline, are recommended by two people sensitive to important life issues -Joseph Campbell and Elisabeth Kubler-Ross.

Joseph Campbell, teacher, writer, and scholar, has spent a lifetime comparing the various religious beliefs throughout the world and through various historical periods. In the book, The Way to Enlightenment, he asks,

"What is the ultimate spiritual discipline?" His answers: "Enjoy your friends." He phrases it this way:

> And what then is finally the best austerity, what is the best discipline? The best discipline is: Enjoy your friends, Enjoy your meals. Realize what your play is. Participate in the play, in the play of life. This is known as mahasukha, the great delight. So there comes this final saying, Bhoga is yoga. Delight and enjoyment (bhoga) is a form of yoga. That is the whole theme of T. S. Eliot's The Cocktail Party. You've got to give a party? That's your ritual, to realize the presence. It's a wonderful thing. That's the great Buddhism. (1990, p.119)

Dr. Elisabeth Kubler-Ross is the author of the landmark work, On Death and Dying, the book which several decades ago began the process of confronting ours as a death-denying culture. Since then she has written numerous books on death including Death, the Final Stage of Growth and To Live Until We Say Good- bye. What is her recommendation on how to live as fully as you possibly can? Appreciation.

It is difficult, if not impossible, at some stages of grief to appreciate what you do have left, especially during the time when your anger is at its peak. But when the storm subsides, moments of appreciation arise.

I can make a list of everything I cherish. It consists of personal things like my family, my friends, my home and the things in it. Beyond that, I appreciate the birds of the air, particularly white birds. Soaring high about me, they seem to be creatures who remind me of my own spiritual nature. I also appreciate trees. Rooted deeply in Mother Earth, their branches reach into the sky. Trees serve to remind me of the connection between this life and the next. The blue sky of day and the stars at night have the power to inspire appreciation for the wonder of life itself and our place in the universe.

When anger subsides, most survivors are able to appreciate what they still have in this world and even begin to be grateful for the time they had with the loved one who died.

PARADOXICAL ADVICE

Further advice on what helps appears in the chapters ahead: "How Do You Deal With Others?" and "What About Holidays?". Here, I would like to make some brief statements regarding the paradoxical nature of things. Most of the really valuable advice I have gotten on any subject is seemingly contradictory until I came to see how each half of a paradox is true in a specific way. The challenge is to discover the particular way in which each half of the paradox is true. Here are some examples:

1. ***Keep up traditions****. Continue the ones that are meaningful and manageable for you.* ***Do things differently****. Your life is different; go with the change, and honor it by creating new traditions.*

2. ***Express your anger****. Anger is legitimate and you have a right to it.* ***Avoid hurting others unnecessarily****. There is a lot of unavoidable pain during grief. You will not want to create any extra for yourself or for others.*

3. ***Spend time alone****. Times when you have little energy, you probably won't want to see anyone.* ***Spend time with others****. You need to talk and to get emotional support from many people.*

4. ***Stay home****. If you feel rooted in your home, it is a source of strength.* ***Get out of town****. There are times when being in your car and going somewhere is the most therapeutic thing you can do.*

5. *There is one piece of paradoxical advice that is so important it needs to be dealt with at length.* ***Avoid making major decisions*** *and,* ***trust your deepest intuition when making daily plans****.*

Avoid Making Major Decisions

After Ben died, Garry talked about selling our house and moving away from everything that reminded him of Ben. Many years ago I heard about the book Widow in which the author, Lynn Cain, cautioned people against making any major decisions for at least one year after the death. You will find you are not always thinking clearly during the grief process. In the throes of this highly emotional time, you are not always as logical as you were in the past or will be again in the future. Furthermore, you are going through a major life transition, and you have no way of knowing what you will be like or what you will want after this transition. Always remember, if there are changes you want to make, you can still do it after a year or 18 months has passed. As my father used to say, "If something is really a good idea now, it will still be a good idea later."

After making this generalization, I also want to reiterate everyone is different and there are no absolutes. Approximately one year after Ben's death, a boy who lived close to us also died. His parents decided they couldn't remain in their house and they put it up for sale. I remember praying at night that the house would not sell, but it did, and for that family, getting rid of the house was exactly the right thing for them to do. Coincidentally, another member of our grief support group put her house up for sale soon after her son's death, but it didn't sell. She was initially disappointed when she could not get rid of her house, but now says she is glad it did not sell. I have a hunch sometimes God intervenes in matters like this. The person who is supposed to make a major change will be given the opportunity to do so. The person who isn't supposed to make the change often is not able to do so. It also seems that divine intervention does not always occur and I have heard some tragic stories about people who make unfortunate decisions after a loss. Here is an example I heard during a lecture for owners of small businesses.

The presenter told a story of a widow who opened a dress shop after her husband's death. Struggling to find a way to give meaning to a life without her spouse, she felt inspired to be of some service to her community. She decided to lift the spirits of the other women in her small lumber town by developing a first class boutique. Procuring a loan from a bank by using her home as collateral, she leased a building, refurbished it using expensive materials, and decorated it with equally high quality furnishings. She then stocked the store with inventory. The store was a treat for the eye, but the business failed. When she lost her business, she also lost her home.

Objective analysis of the boutique as a business in that location would have told her she needed to sell a minimum of two fancy dresses each year to every man, woman and child in her small lumber town if she were to meet expenses and pay herself a modest salary. Consequently, her chances for success were zero from the start.

I heard this story several years before Ben died, but it made me furious. I angrily asked the presenter about the ethics of the banker who made the loan. This actually was the point of the story. The bank official in the town was not so much unethical as he was inexperienced. Conservative people who say "no" to a bereaved person who want to make a major decision too soon in their grief process sometimes do them a favor. This is especially true when the decision does not appear to be in the best interest of the bereaved. A wiser banker might have had the widow do more research into her project before she went ahead. Some paper and pencil cash flow calculations might have prevented her from losing her home as well as her husband.

It is important, however, not to be too discouraging to anyone in bereavement. People need to think seriously about what they can do in the future to make the rest of their life meaningful. The widow in the story bravely faced the fact that her life was going to be different, and had come up with an idea of what she wanted to do with it. Rather than totally discouraging her from pursuing her dream of working in a boutique or conversely being totally supportive of her impractical idea of opening the boutique in a small lumber town, the banker might have suggested she get a job at someone else's boutique in a nearby city. She could start to do what she really wanted and learn something about that type of business before she opened one of her own. Common sense tells us that some experience is desirable, perhaps even essential, before attempting a risky venture. If the banker would have suggested proper planning, this advice to the widow would not have been different from what is advisable to anyone thinking about entering a business. The use of common sense can guide our thinking about what is helpful and what is unwise.

Like the widow in the lumber town, I too wanted to do something after Ben's death to make my life more meaningful. Being a conservative person, I did not quit my job. Instead, I did a lot of writing in my spare time. There is fortunately a difference between writing rough drafts in your free time and having it accepted for publication. About one year after Ben's death I sent off one of my manuscripts. Since rejection is more common in the publishing business than acceptance, I expected to receive a rejection letter. When I got mine in the mail, I wasn't surprised. The draft did need revision before it would become a publishable piece of work.

The big change I wanted to make in my life required lots of time. Doing more research, rewriting the manuscripts several times, proofreading each time, getting suggestions for revision from people with editing skills, getting opinions from friends who read the manuscript, and getting an analysis of the draft from medical professions all took years to accomplish. It was a blessing in disguise because it slowed me down from acting too quickly and doing something I would later regret. Thank heavens I got an original "no." My manuscript was ultimately a worthwhile project, but unlike the widow from the lumber town, I was forced to wait a number of years before sharing my ideas with the public.

Irreversible decisions should also be made with caution when possible. I am glad I made few irreversible decisions after Ben's death because I have more options today. Here is an example: Two days after Ben died, I went through his room to deal with his belongings. I have lots of storage space in the garage, so I could put everything in boxes. I did not want to part with anything, but I also did not want his room kept as it had been.

Now, four years later, as I am feeling distant from Ben, I can bring a part of him closer to me by opening those boxes. In the future I may want to unpack a few of his shirts, make some changes to them, and wear them myself. I could decorate them with iron-on decals or a design. To add color and brightness, I might use fabric paints and glitter. It may give me a warm, comfortable feeling to wear his clothes which I have also made personally mine through craftwork. But if it turns out to be painful instead of comforting, I can just return his shirts to their boxes and put them back on the shelf. My plan of making alterations to some of his shirts may not be a good one, but at least I have the option of trying it because I still have them.

Making irreversible decisions limits your options, whereas knowing there are many choices available allows you to feel that life is expanding. My example of keeping Ben's shirts is not meant to imply that sharing the property of the deceased is not a good idea. For other people, giving away the clothing was a meaningful thing to do. Using their intuition—what felt right for them—they were guided to give things away, either to close friends of the deceased who cherished the items, or to a worthy cause. There are no absolutes. The point is, allow yourself the option of having choices.

Follow your deepest intuition in making daily decisions.

Because of the paradoxical nature of life, no one can tell anyone what is best for them. Well meaning friends may tell you that you need to come to their party to forget your problems for a while. Sometimes these friends are right. After listening to them, you may want to tell them you appreciate the invitation and you will come if you can. You probably won't know until the day of the party itself if you'll actually attend or not. In this situation the adage, "take one day at a time," is appropriate.

Each day you can respect the wisdom within you by asking yourself, "What do I need to do <u>this</u> day?" If you trust your intuition, it will likely tell you exactly what will help. One day when I just did not know what to do, I had a feeling that I really needed to re-organize my closet. It may sound silly, but it was precisely the thing that made me feel better. I was doing something very personal, something just for myself. Putting something of my outer life in order helped to put something of my inner self in order as well.

How Do You Deal With Other People?

Before Ben's death, I imagined that if someone very close to me died, my grief would be just an exaggerated form of the sorrow everyone else felt. When my father died, I felt grief, but it was far from devastating. I loved him dearly, but somehow I didn't perceive his death as a dramatic loss. I do not know why I reacted as I did, but I believe it was precisely because he was such a good father and taught me to be independent that I didn't think, "What in the world am I going to do without him?" When my sister died of a rheumatic heart condition, I was indirectly affected by her death, via my mother's grief. Being only four years old, I had few memories of her myself and felt little direct grief from her death.

When a child, spouse, significant other, or sibling you are especially close to or a parent upon whom you rely dies, your grief may be little understood by others who have no experience of profound loss. My grief over Ben's death certainly came as a surprise to me. How can you explain to others about the period of shock when you are protected from the longer lasting grief work which comes months later? What do others need to know about what you are going through, so they can treat you appropriately?

LOWER EXPECTATIONS

People should not expect much from you for a long time. You do not have the energy or the ability to work at your full potential. Getting up each day and going to work is, however, more helpful than discontinuing work. Tolerance from others is what is required. Fellow workers and friends need to know that recovery takes 2-3 years, not 4-5 months.

Similarly, you can not expect too much from others. Friends and co-workers can give you some support and can help you at times, but if you lean on too few people too heavily or too long, they simply can't take it. They want to help and are willing to do what they can, but you have extra needs that require a variety of resources.

ANGER

Anger is a natural reaction to having been hurt. Suicide survivors have been hurt as badly as anyone can be. We are angry, and we are looking for a target for this anger. I tried not to take my anger out on my friends. Instead, I took it out on my car. Each time I got in or out of my automobile, I used it as an opportunity to slam the door just as hard as I could. Some of the doors in my house got the same treatment.

It is hard, however, not to occasionally target our anger at others. Mad at the whole world, we are easily offended by relatively benign comments like the greeting, "Hi, how are your doing?" We would like to scream, "How in the (expletive) do you think I'm doing? I hurt like (expletive)." Instead we probably lie and say, "Fine." When family or friends encounter a suicide survivor or anyone who has experienced a loss, they might consider saying something like, "Hi! It's good to see you!"

The whole issue of how you can interact with others, and how they can interact with you, is complex. In some cultures, leaving the person alone is the honored custom. During bereavement, persons are naturally angry and the community knows they are likely to do hurtful things they would not do under usual circumstances. Anger makes them overly-sensitive and easily hurt. I hesitate to criticize friends who chose to leave the bereaved alone during their grief. There are some sound reasons for doing so. But in our culture when something is ignored, the interpretation is either that what happened is not important or that friends do not have the necessary commitment to you to help when you need it.

Family and friends who wish to acknowledge the importance of what has happened to you and express how important you are to them will want to choose a method that feels comfortable for them. When this is thoughtfully done it is likely to be comfortable for you as well.

CRYING

A suicide survivor, or anyone in bereavement, generally does not want to be put in the position of crying in public. There are some exceptions to this. I remember crying at the Orlando airport and it did not embarrass me in the least. No one in Orlando knew me, and airports are one of those places where typically people cry. The tears that came over me suddenly regarding Ben's death were indistinguishable from those of others at the airport who were saying good-bye to loved ones. Breaking into tears at the neighborhood grocery store, on the other hand, is not something I want to do. Lots of people know me there. Even though they are all very nice and would have been more than sympathetic, breaking down in public there would have embarrassed me.

Sparing the survivor the embarrassment of crying in public while at the same time acknowledging them in a special way is difficult. I remember how the husband of one of my friends was able to do it. One evening the monthly get-together of the eight members of our bridge group was at his house. He walked through the living room to do what most husbands do on those occasions—say a brief hello and help himself to some of the refreshments. As he was making congenial remarks to everyone, he unobtrusively put his hand on my shoulder for a second.   That momentary human touch communicated what words could not. In that public setting it did not reduce me to tears. It is often these simple, subtle, thoughtful gestures that are appreciated and never forgotten.

The bereaved do need to talk and to cry about what has happened, but in a private setting where they feel safe. When you are in your own home or at a friend's house, in the presence of one other person or a small intimate group, crying is therapeutic. In a private setting; friends who say something to survivors which causes them to cry need not feel they have done something to make them feel bad. The bereaved feels bad <u>all</u> of the time during the most painful times of grief work.   Your innocent remark only serves to make their pain more visible by bringing forth the tears that are always there even when they are not flowing.

I recall being at a friend's house when she said some little thing that made me cry. Quickly coming to my side, she put her arms around me, saying she had not meant to hurt me. I did not explain to her at the time, but I remember thinking how silly of her to assume her totally innocent remark would have hurt me. I was walking around constantly fighting back tears. What she said had nothing to do with my crying; it was just a catalyst starting a natural flow of tears. We were in the privacy of her home. I was not embarrassed to cry; it was therapeutic for me to do so.

CARDS, LETTERS, PHONE CALLS

I have never heard a suicide survivor say they were offended when a friend or family member sent them a "thinking of you" card. A little thing like that is a very thoughtful way of saying they care about you but hesitate to invade your privacy at a time when you may not have the energy to cope with company.

Family members or friends can also write simple letters. No one <u>has</u> to find just the right card to express what they feel. They are perfectly capable of expressing it themselves. A message of concern need only take the cost of a postage stamp. One need not go shopping. A short, simple note will give as much comfort to a survivor as anything else you can do.

When my sister Ellen died, her teacher had every children in her schoolroom write my parents a letter. My mother is not the type of person who saves anything. Part of her system of keeping our farmhouse immaculately neat and clean was to avoid clutter. She got rid of anything that was not absolutely necessary, but she did save those letters. Their location in the right side of the bottom drawer of her dresser was well known to every child in our family.

What a thoughtful thing for that teacher to do! This simple act gave each child a means of expressing their own feeling about the death, while giving something very precious to my parents—a gift they treasured through the years. My brothers and sisters recognized them as valuable to the healing process for our entire family.

Some people find   using the telephone easier, more natural and comfortable, than using the mail. Friends need to do what is best for them. They will probably also come to learn what means of communication you appreciate the most. If you welcome those calls, saying "thank you for calling" lets them know that you would like them to do it more often.

THE WORST QUESTION ANYONE CAN ASK

During the first year or so of your bereavement, the worst question anyone can ask a bereaved parent is, "How many children do you have?" (You can imagine what the counterpart to that would be if the suicide victim were your spouse, or your sibling, but I will use the example of a parent here to streamline the writing of this section.)

How do you answer a question like that? If you leave the suicide victim out, you may feel you are negating his or her rightful place in your life and in your family. When wrestling with the problem of how to answer this question, parents sometimes feel they will be disloyal to the deceased child if they do not include him or her in their answer.

Personally, when I have been forced to answer that question by including my son, I break into tears. This happened to me when I went to a specialist and the doctor did a medical history.   He asked two separate questions: "How many pregnancies did you have?" and "How many children do you have?" He asked these questions approximately six months after

Ben died—during the worst part of my grief. I was so upset I'm afraid <u>he</u> never quite recovered from the experience.

There is no right answer to how to handle these questions. The response you give may even change over time. You will want to think about what makes you most comfortable at each stage of your grief. I do not want to cry in public, so when I am asked about my children, I just talk about my daughter. I do not feel I am hiding the fact Ben died by suicide, for I have no shame regarding the cause of his death. I do not feel I am being disloyal to him. It is just that the stranger who asks me the question <u>is</u> a stranger. My son is very precious to me and his life brings forth strong emotions within me I do not necessarily wish to display with every new person I meet.

One of the reasons bereaved people feel uncomfortable in settings where they will meet new people is because they typically get asked questions like, "What does your husband do?," or "How many children do you have?" I know it is the case for me even now, five years later. Part of the reason for avoiding social situations where you will encounter new people is you may not have decided how you want to answer those questions. You will learn to tailor your answer to fit the situation.

WHAT DO YOU TELL OTHERS ABOUT HOW THE SUICIDE VICTIM DIED?

At the time of Ben's death, I was straightforward with most people about the fact of his suicide. The thought of being secretive about the cause of death never seriously crossed my mind. Trying to keep a secret takes more energy than I had, and I did not see any benefits from it. In contrast, telling the truth over and over again is healing.

A staff person at one of our group homes for mentally retarded adults wanted to know what they should tell the clients about Ben's death. I had two concerns. First, I was not sure if I would be doing them a favor by presenting them with an image of someone they knew using a gun to shoot himself in the head. Second, I wanted to protect myself from anything they might say to me which would hurt. I love my clients but to say all of them are tactful or sophisticated would not be accurate.

I never lie to them, but there are times when omitting some details is appropriate. Thinking about this issue and talking it over with a staff member, I concluded that since Ben shot himself, fell, and died, it would be truthful to simply omit the first phrase and tell the developmentally disabled clients that Ben fell and died. Our clients were not unnecessarily excluded from what had happened to Ben. They attended the visitation at the funeral home the night before the funeral. They are an integral part of our lives, and they too were given an opportunity to say good-bye to their friend.

Some of their most precious memories of Ben are associated with outings to our little cabin by the lake. When we took them to the cabin after his death, they often talked about Ben and the many things he would do for them to make those trips fun. One time when the clients were talking of him, one of the women told the others to stop talking about Ben because "it made Garry and Trudy feel bad." I assume the woman's mother had been concerned, as I had been, about the clients saying things that would hurt us. Recalling pleasant memories of the deceased is not something that hurts a survivor, but I am grateful to that mother for wanting to spare me unnecessary pain.

YOUNG CHILDREN AND SUICIDE

I recall hearing a survivor angrily telling a story of a group of young children who were playing suicide. After a death in the community, the youngsters were pretending to shoot themselves, fall down and get up laughing. The survivor telling the story assumed the children were following the example of adults in the town who were making fun of the deceased. I am not sure her assumption was correct.

Infants learn about the world by putting everything they see into their mouths. Young children learn to understand and cope with things that happen in their lives by playing. Children are so full of energy and joy it is only natural for them to laugh while they play. Had I seen those children playing suicide after the death of my son, I too would have been terribly hurt and bitterly angry. But in reality it is not their fault they are in the developmental stage in which they use play to integrate new information. I am sure the parents would have been horrified that something their children did in all innocence hurt someone's feelings. Luckily for me, I was spared an incident like that.

Parents want to understand the effect the death has on children. Some bereaved parents come to our suicide support group specifically to find answers to their questions regarding how they can best help their surviving children. They want to know if there is something special they need to do; if there are particular problems their children will have, and if there is anything they should avoid doing.

There has not been much research on young children who have lost someone to suicide. We need to rely on the general grief literature to give us some insights. Since suicide survivors are more like other bereaved people than they are different, using this information has general validity. Much of what I learned was from a lecture by William Worden at the 1991 conference of the American Death Education Association. Worden made these important points.

1.   *Children have different grieving behaviors than adults.*

It is not at all unusual for a child to go up to a total stranger and tell the person about the death in the family. Children also often ask the same questions over and over again. Even though you may have thoroughly answered their question the first time, children want to know that the story has not changed. Answering it each time may hurt you deeply, but children have a need to keep asking.

Children will play death games. When I was a child we liked to play church. After a funeral, it is not abnormal for children to want to play funeral.

In adolescence, young people may not show sadness around their family. Many teens prefer to express their feelings to their closest friends and to their girlfriends or boyfriends.

Since adolescence is the stage when young people need to develop independence and strong peer relationships, it makes sense that they would do their primary grief work with people their own age. My own daughter was willing to be a support for me, but I gave her no support myself. She was a beginning college student when Ben died and began seeing friends who had or were in the process of experiencing a loss. Everyone is different and she did what was right for her to do.

2.   *Children may take longer to grieve than adults.*

Children have fewer developmental coping skills than do adults; consequently, they are not always able to handle the sophisticated tasks of the grief process at the time the loss occurs. It is common for a person to grieve over a childhood loss years later, especially during mid-life. Children can not grieve intensely and often re-experience grief during each separate developmental stage. For example, if a parent died when the child was young, they may go through grief during their early teens when the missing parent can not attend their first game, in later teens when the parent is not there to see them go to the prom, or enter college, and in early adulthood when the parent is not there to see them get married, or share the joy holding their first child.

3.   *There are many questions on the minds of children who have lost a parent or sibling.*

These questions include, "Did I cause it to happen?" During the magical age of three to five, children believe that if they think something, it could happen. If children were ever angry at the deceased, it could translate into: "I was so mad I wanted them gone and now they are. It's all my fault." Children may never share their fears and guilt about the death. The parent may want to talk to them and let them know it is common for children to think they are responsible, when they really are not.

Another question children have is, "Will it happen to me?" Again, children may not express their concern to the parent, and the adult will need to take the initiative to talk about this with children. The other poignant question youngsters have is, "Who is going to take care of me?" Young children need some reassurance that they will be taken care of. Giving them a list which would include the surviving parent, grandparents or aunts and uncles or closest friend may be enough to reassure children they will be taken care of. During the grief process, surviving parents are sometimes in such pain themselves they are emotionally unavailable to their surviving children. In our community we have support groups for children who have lost someone. This seems to be helpful to meet some of the emotional needs of those youngsters.

The parent who has lost a child to suicide often wonders if the death will have a negative effect on the surviving children.

FACTORS AFFECTING CHILDREN'S
REACTION TO LOSS

1.   *The level of cognitive and emotional development of the children.*

The children who have trouble putting their feelings into words may have a difficult time with grief. Parents may want to help them with this. I always find I can talk better when I walk. Going for a walk and talking might be helpful, or perhaps talking after a workout, playing ball, or some other shared activity might work best.

2.   *Magical thinking*

As mentioned earlier, very young children may feel responsible for the death and need reassurance that they are not to blame. When my sister died I was developmentally in the magic years of 3-5 years old. I do not recall feeling responsible for her death, but I felt it was my responsibility to <u>fix</u> the problem. My mother was grieving, and it was up to me to take away her pain.

3.   *Children need social support in every aspect of their lives.*

Just as adults need all the friends they can get during grief, so do children. Since the parent or parents are devastated by the loss, it is helpful when other close family members or close friends step in to give children extra attention during the first years after the death. If children are in school, teachers can do a lot to help them. They can give children reassurance that they know they are going through a difficult time. Teachers can even enlist the help of a few sensitive and mature students to be especially helpful and supportive.

Particularly during adolescence, the surviving teens need all the help they can get from peers. Again the school can be of some assistance here. Often a school counselor needs to take the initiative to ensure they get the support that is needed. If these adolescents have strong communication skills, they might be able to enlist the needed support on their own. Resourceful teens can do a lot to help themselves. The counselor needs to assess how capable each adolescent is in obtaining the support they need. If the teens are getting it on their own, then they may only need to check in with the counselor every once in a while. But if the adolescent is not getting the help needed, the counselor may need to take the lead.

4.   The previous mental health condition of the children

If the surviving children also have a depressive illness or anxiety disorder, this loss will add additional stress. Depression is the common cold of mental health. If a parent or sibling commits suicide, it does not mean the surviving children also have a depressive illness that will be fatal. But it is worth asking the question, "Do the surviving children also have a milder case of depression?" These children need to be evaluated. Furthermore, depression is a cyclical condition. One evaluation does not necessarily mean the onset of depression will not occur six months, one year, two, three, or even four years later. It only makes sense to re-evaluate any time you become concerned especially if you see changes in the children's behavior such as social withdrawal, destructive behaviors, persistent anxiety, frequent accidents, the development of illegal behaviors such as stealing, promiscuity, eating problems, or sleeping disturbance. Take these as red flags and get an evaluation for depression or anxiety. The children may need help.

5. *Ambivalent feelings about their relationship with the deceased*

If the person who committed suicide was especially irritable or angry, the survivor's memories of the deceased is that he or she was difficult to get along with. The surviving children may have loved the deceased but may be justifiably angry at many of the things he or she did or said. Youngsters need reassurance that it is natural to feel this way, and they can be encouraged to express those feelings in whatever way they feel comfortable: talking about it with family or peer, writing about it, etc.

6. *Re-defining or re-assigning the child's role in the family*

After the death, one surviving child may take on a new role. If the father committed suicide, the oldest boy may now become "the man in the family." Taking on an adult role is more than can be expected of any child. Although roles will naturally shift and everyone will be changed after the shattering loss of a family member, it is not necessary or fair to expect one children to fill the void created by a death.

7.   Unstable or inconsistent environments

Consistent rules and reliable routines provided by emotionally stable parents produce a sense of security for children. Change of any kind produces some stress. The death of a family member is a major change which adds a substantial amount of stress. If the children have a chaotic home, (one in which life is already difficult) the death will add even more instability to their world. Chaotic families have less resources with which to cope with added stress. Children from unstable homes will need a great deal of ongoing help. Where will this come from? It could come from friends and relatives, or from religious and community social services. Unfortunately, all too often children from chaotic homes do not get as much help as they need.

8.   The vulnerability of the surviving parent

If children have one stable parent, they will be able to rely on that adult. Even though the parent may be temporarily unavailable because of grief, this adult will provide enough care to the children to get them through the crisis. If children do not have one stable parent, the community needs to be aware that these children are at risk.

The literature on grief describes some specific ways to help children during the grief process. It begins by defining the major needs children have:

1. information that is clear and comprehensible
2. involvement and feeling important

3. *reassurance about adult bereavement (why the surviving parent is acting the way he or she is)*
4. *honor one's thoughts and feelings*
5. *maintain interest in one's own age appropriate activities*
6. *express good-bye to the deceased*
7. *memorialize the deceased*

From this list of needs, you can probably make your own list of what children need to do. If you have allowed children to be actively involved in making choices at the time of the funeral, you have already begun meeting their needs during grief. Even if this was not the case, there is still much that can be done. One thing parents have found helpful is to encourage their children to make a memory book of the deceased. The use of pictures and writing about those pictures will become a treasure to the entire family.

Most important of all, however, is for the surviving parent to be a model of normative grief. By this I do not mean you need to be perfect. We are human beings, and human beings are not perfect. A model of normal human behavior will be a model of our imperfections, our pain, and our problems. Our children will love us and respect us for our human nature. They can not relate to inhuman perfection. Therefore, our children need to see us cry and learn it is all right for adults to show their feelings. But young children will also need to feel our strength. They still need the security of rules and limits that are enforced. Children want the safety of routine in their life, rather than total chaos. They need reassurance and lots of hugs—things you undoubtedly do every day.

Do not be surprised if your children develop a number of temporary problems during the first months after a death. You can expect to see somatic symptoms such as headaches and stomach aches, some anxiety, probably some aggression and school problems. After all, they are going to have pain and anger similar to what you are feeling with your grief. These symptoms will likely subside after four or five months. It is only when they do not subside or get worse over time that there is a reason for concern. After all, your grief has it's own cyclical nature. Your children's does, too.

Before Ben's death I did not have the slightest idea how to react to a person who had lost someone dear to them. I would express my sympathy at the time of the death, but would give little thought to the continuing effect the loss has on the life of my friend or relative. Grief is a powerful teacher. From it we can learn to be more careful in how we deal with others.

What About Holidays?

A ny special day is potentially painful for the bereaved. My writing reflects my experience. I was raised in the Christian tradition and in the United States. Consequently, the chapter focuses on holidays such as Christmas and Thanksgiving. My omission of the special days of other traditions is not meant to denigrate their importance. It is simply that I could not write with any authority about customs not in my experience. I do not wish to treat them with less respect than I actually have for those traditions by writings that would necessarily lack genuine insight.

CHRISTMAS

Christmas will never be the same again. It is the day when everyone in the family is supposed to be home. After a suicide, the absence of that member of your family is acutely painful. Questions arise like, "How many stockings do you hang?" "What do you do with the special ornaments bought for the deceased or which remind you of him or her?" How can any of us approach what is supposed to be the season of joy when our emotions are anything but joyful?

The Christmas cards, the shopping for gifts, the baking and cooking, decorating the tree and the house, plus entertaining, can be exhausting, if not overwhelming, for anyone. During grief, doing it all is an unreasonable expectation. Although there is no generalization absolutely true for everyone, most survivors do find it helpful to either streamline existing family traditions, create new ones, or both.

Family decisions made with the input of all members are effective. Make a list of what is essential and what is not. Come up with ideas for what can be delegated to any surviving children. This lifts the burden off the shoulders of the surviving parent or parents.

The Tree

The Christmas tree is usually on the top of the list of essentials. If there are older children in the family who can drive, they probably would be happy to buy the tree. All the children could then trim it. If it does not look as picture perfect as it did in years past, no one really cares, and the children will feel proud of their contribution. If some ornaments are too painful to look at, they could be put aside for a year or for the next couple of years. Perhaps you would like to trim the tree with a few new ornaments or all new ornaments. Let your intuition be your guide about what to do with the tree. If a tree is not essential, some people like to buy poinsettias to add some color to the home.

Stockings

If hanging individual stockings has been your custom, get family input on whether or not to exclude the stocking of the deceased. Maybe you want to put up the others and put a candle where his or her stocking would have been. Perhaps you just want to skip the stocking this year or from now on.

Cookies

Christmas cookies could be handled in a similar fashion as the tree. Children are never too young to learn how to cook. If cookies are on the list of essentials, then those family members who really want cookies can make them. Older siblings may need to help younger ones. If the cookies do not turn out picture perfect, who cares? As my mother used to say, "They'll look the same in your stomach." Or maybe you have a relative who doesn't know what to get you for Christmas this year. How about a huge box of homemade cookies?

Cards

If sending Christmas cards does not make the list of essentials, friends and relatives will undoubtedly understand if you choose not to send any. The principle here is to decide what is really meaningful for ourselves and those we love. Sending Christmas cards is something very meaningful to me. I used it as an opportunity to send a thank you letter to my brothers and sisters and a few of my closest friends who were so supportive of me during my bereavement. I had been so concentrated on my own pain, it was not until Christmas time I realized how much pain Ben's death had caused others. I hand wrote one letter and made several copies. It was an opportunity for me to express my gratitude and my growing awareness that the past few months had not been easy for them either. Friends who were not as close just did not get a card that year.

Shopping

Christmas shopping can be especially painful. Just being in the stores may be more than you can handle, particularly if your loved one liked to shop. Streamline, delegate, or both. You can do more exchanging of names, give cash or gift certificates, or order from catalogs.

Parties

How much entertaining you can participate in will depend on you. If your energy is high and keeping busy works for you, this is your season! However, many bereaved find social situations uncomfortable and prefer to decline invitations.

I found I could not be sure if I was going to have a good day or a bad day. I preferred not to make any definite commitments to anything. If I felt like going some place, I went. If I did not feel like going, I did not. People who are really good friends will understand. People who are insensitive are not the kind of people you want in your life anyway.

Service to Others

My life situation is a little different than most. As the operator of small group homes for mentally retarded adults, I think of Christmas as a time when I am especially busy creating a family holiday for those clients who no longer have family. Holidays are, in fact, not a day off for Garry and me to spend with our own children. They are days when we take care of the residents who are at the group homes rather than at their day programs. I can and have worked Christmas day, doing something meaningful and rewarding.

During the five years preceding Ben's death, it had been our practice to schedule our annual Florida vacation during Christmas. It insured that our winter trip would occur when school was closed. Since Ben's death, we have preferred to go to Florida earlier in December and be back at home working during the holiday season. Our new way of spending Christmas is, in many respects, a recapturing of a classical tradition. Being at home in the snowy north, we began an emphasis on service to others rather than focusing on ourselves. Doing things for others during the holidays makes us feel needed and useful, while reminding us we are not the only ones who have had to cope with difficulties in life.

Church

What about church services? If your usual church service is uncomfortable, consider either going to church at a different time or going to a different church. I find going to church uncomfortable. I can not stand seeing all those happy families. Church is also one of those public places that makes me cry. Walking out of the service can be fairly conspicuous. If you are someone who feels comforted at church, by all means stay with it. Do not unnecessarily break contact with the friends you have there and the support you find there. Do what feels good, what works.

Travel

Taking a trip at Christmas time can provide a means of doing something completely different. It is an option well worth serious consideration. If you have younger children, the decision of where to go should be made with their input. If they go somewhere they do not like, not only have they lost their loved one, they will also be cheated out of Christmas. If there are not children involved, go someplace you had always wanted to go.

The weeks before a special day are often more difficult than the actual day itself. With that in mind, Garry and I scheduled a trip the first year for December 5 - 15. Getting out of town, getting away from it all, was helpful to us. Nothing could take away our pain. I can not say the trip was fun, but we felt it was better than being at home.

THANKSGIVING

When someone you loved so much dies, do you have any reason to feel thankful at Thanksgiving? Three, four, or five years from now, you might again see a reason, but the first years may be filled with anger and sorrow rather than gratitude.

Going back to the principle of doing what is meaningful for yourself and those you love, make some changes. Getting through Thanksgiving may mean having dinner at a different place or with different people. It takes some planning to think about what can make this holiday more bearable. Some families may want to go to a restaurant rather than eating at home. Others will want to accept an invitation to eat at someone else's house. Perhaps you might want to eat at home as usual, but instead of feeling diminished because of the absence of the deceased, fill up the seats at your table with one guest or several. Maybe one of your older children has a friend who would appreciate being included or knows of a international student who would enjoy being at a home rather than in the empty dorm. Do you know a widow, a widower, or a divorced person who could use an invitation for a big meal rather than celebrating alone on Thanksgiving? Maybe members of your support group would like to spend Thanksgiving together. You could make it a special time to deliberately deal with the grief you feel.

MOTHER'S DAY/FATHER'S DAY

In writing about this topic, I will simplify it by referring only to Mother's Day. Being a mother myself, the writing will be more natural. I trust the fathers who read this can translate what is relevant for them.

I apologize to all of you who find this special day meaningful. I find it a pain in the neck. Mother's Day can give us an opportunity to acknowledge the love and gratitude we have for our mothers. I prefer to show my love spontaneously throughout the year rather than do it sentimentally once a year.

Mother's Day can be especially painful to a bereaved parent and burdensome for the surviving children. These children feel a responsibility to make their mother happy on that day, when in all likelihood she will spend some, if not most, of the day in tears. All this will make the children feel they have failed. It also underscores the reality that although she has other children, she can not help but focus her attention on the child who has died.

I reject Mother's Day with its commercialism which tries to persuade me to observe it by buying cards, flowers, and gifts. I have the power to say "No" to messages trying to convince me there is only one way to observe the day. Let's look at the day historically.

The first Mother's Day was a protest march by women objecting to the mandatory drafting of soldiers into the Civil War. Mothers who had already lost sons in battle and mothers whose sons could die or be seriously wounded were saying, "No!" In recent years we have taken a day commemorating the angry protests of courageous women and turned it into an opportunity for florists and greeting card companies to do a lot of business. I have nothing against buying flowers and sending cards. Quite the contrary! I highly recommend sending them to the mothers of a suicide victim. But you can do it any day of the year, not just the second Sunday in May.

It might help the suicide survivor to change the focus from herself as an individual, to the mother we all share: Mother Earth. Nature is a healing force. Consider spending the day walking in the woods, planting a tree, digging in a flower bed, sitting by an ocean, lake or stream, climbing a hill, or whatever nature experience gives you peace.

THE LOVED ONE'S BIRTHDAY /
THE ANNIVERSARY OF THE DEATH

These days can be some of the hardest. Any of the suggestions already made for dealing with special days such as getting out of town, spending time with Mother Nature, or doing something different, are appropriate here. Family members or close friends may wish to make a public recognition of the day by: ordering flowers for the altar at church, buying a book to place in a school or public library as a memorial, or donating money to a favorite charity in the name of the deceased.

Some of my friends sent presents to us on Ben's birthday. One person cross-stitched the poem another friend had written at the time of my son's death. (A typed copy of the poem was given to everyone who attended the funeral service. She saved her copy, stitching the poem onto fabric, added some decorative touches, had it framed, and gave it to us on Ben's birthday.) Another friend sent us flowers. If you are the friend of a survivor you may want to send a card or do something special on the anniversary of the death or on the deceased's birthday, or any day. We received a stained glass picture of a butterfly a few months after Ben died from a friend who made it knowing how much it would mean to us.

SPECIAL DAYS THAT TAKE YOU BY SURPRISE

I have little trouble with Christmas, Thanksgiving, Ben's birthday or the anniversary of his death. I have a terrible time with July 4. The day is very difficult for me and I do not know why. Perhaps it is because July 4 is the height of summer fun: the lake is warm enough for swimming and Ben loved the water. He still had two months of summer vacation left to enjoy so there was a comfortable distance between him and his school problems. How Ben loved fireworks! I mention my problem with July 4 because other survivors also find particular special days unexpectedly painful. You are not unusual if you too have days other than the traditional holiday that give you your worst moments.

How Can Suicide Affect You?

T his chapter will examine some of the other ways a suicide death can affect a survivor. I will not sugarcoat the topic by telling you all of the effects will ultimately be positive if you just do your grief work correctly. I firmly believe   benefits   can come if the suffering survivors endure, but there also are potential problems. If you are one of the unlucky people who experience difficulty arising from the suicide, please believe me—it is not your fault! Life just is not fair.

POST TRAUMATIC SHOCK RESPONSE

PTSR (also call Post - Traumatic Stress Disorder) is an anxiety disorder resulting from stress.   Traumatic situations causing PTSR range from natural disasters, wars, sexual or physical assault, and the sudden death of a loved one. Symptoms of PTSR include   loss of appetite, cardiac palpitations, melancholy, nostalgia, anxiety, weakness, fever, and confused thinking.

Most of what is known about PTSR is from men who are veterans of war. Vivid memories of seeing buddies wounded or killed in battle hit the soldier without warning during the day or at night as he sleeps. Ex-soldiers suffering from the condition may need to spend some time in the hospital. Others return to their homes and suffer without help or get treatment from a therapist or support from a group such as vets club.   Some soldiers do not feel the full effect of PTSR until years after discharge. During the American Civil War it was called "battle fatigue" because of the weakness, loss of appetite, melancholia and fever. During WWI it was called "shell shock" because it was believed there was physical trauma to the brain when shells exploded. During both wars, doctors assumed some weakness within the person made them susceptible to PTSR. Consequently, in WWII, it became common practice to screen soldiers to keep those perceived to be susceptible to PTSR out of the armed forces.

There is no evidence that PTSR occurs because of any inherent weakness. During WWII, when screening was done, it still was necessary to permanently discharge 37.5% of soldiers who saw combat because of PTSR. The Korean War and the war in Vietnam have produced as many, if not more, veterans with this condition.

At the heart of PTSR is a diminished capacity to feel. During combat, it is a necessary survival mechanism. In order to survive, the soldier has to go through a radical reduction in his sense of what is actually going on around him. This survival mechanism can work during battle for a number of weeks, months, and even years. But the mechanism usually can not work forever, and many soldiers become affected by the stress of combat sometime after entering the war. Others do not feel the effect until after they return home.

The stress of combat typically affects veterans who report rage, difficulty in intimacy, recurring nightmares, and experiencing disorientation in civilian life. PTSR not only affects the veterans but has reverberations in their families. The term "dysfunctional family" describes their situation. Unable to feel, some veterans may have difficulty being intimate with their wives and might experience some problems having warm interactions with their children.

The veteran feels isolated from others and has difficulty communicating. His anger, irritability, and agitation can be a factor in causing some level of violence in the family. The person has low self-esteem and has diminished ability to cope. He may use alcohol or other drugs in an effort to self-medicate his condition. This, unfortunately, can increase the level of stress or violence in the home.

The sudden trauma of a death by suicide can result in Post Traumatic Shock Response for the survivors. It is helpful for them to recognize and understand the symptoms. While some survivors may experience relatively mild and temporary symptoms, others can have more severe and/or long-lasting effects.

When our son died, my husband found the body. I believe Garry went into shock. He stumbled home to tell me the news. When I informed him I was coming with him to see Ben, he warned me not to come. I emphatically insisted on going. When I entered the room where Ben lay, I stood over the body. Garry knelt down beside it.

In the months that followed the death, we both experienced PTSR symptoms, though mine were less severe. We each had very different experiences of Ben's death. I can not fully explain what caused one of us to suffer more from the disorder while the other was spared, but a partial analysis of the differences between our experience may be helpful to others.

1.   *Finding the body*

Both Garry and I are intuitive people. We realized Ben was upset. We feared the worst. Each of us had separately come to the conclusion Ben might have hurt himself. When Garry went looking for Ben, he knew what he might find. But there is a difference between being worried about someone and actually finding the body. (Even if a loved one has a terminal illness, you still are never prepared to find them dead.) The person who discovers the body always carries an extra burden.

2.   *Alone with the body*

When Garry came to get me he said, "It's Ben." He did not say, "Ben is dead." My intuition told me Ben was dead, rather than lying seriously hurt, still alive. As I entered the room, I too had to learn of Ben's death for the first time. However, I was not alone in that room. I had Garry with me. It is my belief that had I been forced to be alone in the room, as Garry had been a few minutes earlier, I too might have suffered greater trauma.

3.   *Distance from the body*

Garry knelt down close to Ben and touched him. I stood over him, but something very deep within me told me to keep a certain distance. I wish to make it clear here that I am not making any recommendations for anyone else. Everyone needs to do what they need to do in any situation. Garry wanted to be as close to Ben as he possibly could get; he wanted to touch him and to tell him how much he loved him. In my case, something told me it was better not get too close. Ben was my son too, but something within me said this was now just a corpse and something from which I needed to keep a distance.

4.   *The condition of the body*

Though Ben had shot himself, little damage was visible. I believe seeing him was not horrifying, in the usual sense of the word, for either myself or Garry. Some police officers, medical personnel, or family and friends may prevent the people closest to the suicide victim from seeing the body. I believe they do this because they wish to protect the bereaved from suffering from mild or severe forms of Post Traumatic Shock Response if the condition of the body is particularly distressful.

If the body is damaged to the point that it would be horrifying, the judgment is sometimes made that the bereaved is better off not seeing the body right away. The inability to relate to a body is, however, very troublesome for the bereaved. Seeing the body allows the death to become real. When I saw Ben's body on the floor, and even more poignantly in the funeral home, I knew the corpse was not really my son. Ben continued in spirit. His corpse was only a discarded shell. Dealing with a body gave me a foundation for the healing process.

The decision to deny a parent, spouse, child, sibling, or close friend the right to see the body should be made with caution. Often the individuals themselves need to make the decision based on what is best for them. Only the survivor will know if it is better for them to see the body and deal with the shock, than to live the rest of their lives wondering about it. I have heard many survivors express anger at those who denied them the opportunity to see the body of their loved one.

If there has been obvious damage at the time of death, the survivors may need to wait until the mortician has done the best to prepare the body. With some counseling regarding what they can expect to see, and some time to think about what effect it may have on them, they can choose whether or not to view the body.

Even if you do not see the body at the time of the death, the suicide can still produce PTSR. Suicides can shatter previously-held beliefs about yourself and about life itself.

One's sense of security and safety are challenged, causing an increases in the level of anxiety.

Understanding PTSR, as well as the grief process, is important if the suicide survivors are going to comprehend why they are experiencing all the symptoms they do. One support group who studied both PTSR and grief found a combined approach helpful, valid, comfortable, and fit their needs. Members of the groups were grateful for the insights they gained, saying it gave them a useful framework upon which to understand what was happening to them personally and in their family life. Although no system of working with the grief of suicide survivors can take their pain away, integrating the data on PTSR with grief theory can give a means of developing strategies to solve the problems arising from these conditions. Especially in a group setting, members feel they are understood and supported in their efforts to cope with difficult situations.

Post Traumatic Shock Response is not something to be take lightly. Most people recover from it, but if you take an honest look at the records coming from the War Department after a conflict (like our nation's Civil War) you will discover it can do serious and occasionally permanent damage to some people.

DEPRESSION

There is often a genetic predisposition to depressive illness. Suicide survivors who learn for the first time that their deceased loved had a depressive illness, often ask (for good reason), "Do I have a depressive condition myself?" It is both a logical question to ask and one that is difficult to answer.

If the suicide victim is a member of your immediate family, you may not necessarily have a depressive illness yourself, but you are more likely to suffer from it than the general population. Depression is, remember, the common cold of mental illness. At least 10% of the population will have a severe (clinical) depressive episode at least once in their life. An additional 30% of the population will have a moderate or mild case of depression. Experiencing a depression is not in the least unusual. People with this illness are not "crazy." They are, however, in a lot of pain.

If the suicide victim is your child, learning that this illness often has a genetic basis may cause the depressed survivor to think, "Oh my God! I gave this illness to my child!" Thoughts like this increase feelings of guilt, and excessive guilt is a symptom of depression. Little wonder that depressed parents, already overwhelmed by illogical guilt over the death of their child, will feel fresh guilt when confronting the genetic nature of their illness and the illness of the child.

Let's use objective logic to deal with this unnecessary guilt. If you blame yourself for passing this condition on to your child, answer this question: "Where did you get your genes?" We could pass on the blame to the grandparents, but where did they get their genes? You can go back to great-grandparents and great, great grandparents, but let's face it—Adam and Eve have a lot to account for to all of us! Or should the finger of blame be pointed to the ultimate source of everything?

When a survivor is in the throes of painful periods of grief, it is very difficult to tell if what they are experiencing is grief alone, or depression. The symptoms of severe grief include eating problems, sleep disturbance, inability to concentrate, profound sadness for an extended period of time, easily moved to tears, irritability, problems with memory, and low energy. This is exactly what you find in depression. How in the world can anyone tell the difference between grief and a genetically based depression? I do not see how it can be done if you only concentrate on current symptoms. A medical professional needs to get historical information from the bereaved, and from close family members, in order to discover what the person was like in the years preceding the death. If the survivor has a history of past behavior indicative of depression, then there is reason to suspect a recurring unipolar or bipolar depression condition in addition to the grief.

Since depression is terribly painful, and at least 4 out of 5 people respond to current anti-depressant medication, seeking treatment makes sense. No one can take away your grief, but the odds are in your favor that you will get relief from the symptoms of depression.

In addition to using historical data to differentiate grief from genetically based depression conditions, we also need to recognize the existence of reactive depression. Any major loss, such as a death, can cause depression in someone with no previous history of depressive symptoms. How do you tell the difference between grief and a reactive depression? You must look at the length of time the painful grief lasts.

Using my case as an example, my worst time was a four-and-a-half month period from August 13 - December 31. It is similar to what Veninga discovered in his research on loss -- the time from 4 to 8 months after a loss is often the most difficult. If a bereaved person's intense pain lasts a lot longer, a reactive depression may be suspected. Keep in mind that I had times—one week every month or six weeks after the worst period—in which I was back to square one (feeling as devastated as I had at my worst moments). It is not these occasional periods of necessary grief work but non-stop intense pain lasting many months longer than the four month period Veninga described that may be indicative of a reactive depression.

ANXIETY

Like depression, high anxiety can run in families. Just because your mother, father, brother, sister, or child had an anxiety or panic disorder does not necessarily mean you have one, but it does increase your chances. In his book, The Anxiety Disease, Dr. David Sheehan describes the medications used to treat anxiety. Each person's response to medication is unique, but there are some generalizations that can be made. The current medications most effective for anxiety include the antidepressants. According to Dr. Sheehan the family of antidepressants known at the MAO (monoamine oxidase) inhibitors is the most effective medication for anxiety disorder.

The disadvantage of the MAO inhibitors include food restrictions when taking these medications, particularly the elimination of most dairy products. Many individuals adapt easily to these necessary dietary restrictions, but if the person cannot eliminate specific foods from the diet, the medications will not be prescribed. This was true in my son's case. MAO inhibitors was the medication of choice for his combination of anxiety disorder and depressive illness, but I knew Ben, at age thirteen and with his impulsive eating pattern, could not be trusted to stay away from foods like cheese pizza.

Other antidepressants which have no food restrictions are more widely used. They include the tricyclics, such as imipramine and desipramine. Imipramine is the oldest; subsequently, there have been many studies done on it throughout the years. Its effectiveness and possible side effects are well known. Other medications such as trazodone and mianserin are also effective. These medications are not as old as the MAO inhibitors or the tricyclics; consequently, they have not been studied as extensively, but the results thus far are promising as a treatment for anxiety.

These medications have side effects, such as dry mouth, constipation, headaches, dizziness, blurry vision, insomnia, agitation of sedation, which generally are more noticeable during the first weeks. If medications are prescribed for your anxiety, you'll have to be willing to tolerate these side effects. Medications with fewer side effects are also generally less effective. If your anxiety is less severe, a less effective medication with less side effect may work well to meet your needs. The decision as to what medication to use will be based partly on what is required to control the condition. A doctor who has a wide experience with these medications should be able to explain exactly why a particular medication is chosen. Since response to any medication is different for each person, do not be surprised if several are tried before you and your doctor can decide what works best for you.

FURTHER DEATHS

Occasionally I attend a vigil for survivors of suicide which honors the memories of loved ones. Part of the ceremony is the reading of the names of the people who died. The third year this vigil was held, I was awestruck by the common last names of a number of suicide victims. It made it painfully clear to me that depression runs in families and sometimes one suicide can trigger others. It underscored the importance of treating depression.

Getting treatment for depression or anxiety is no guarantee further deaths will not occur. My own son died while getting treatment from a highly competent adolescent psychiatrist. Proper treatment will not necessarily prevent suicide, but it does reduce the risk. This is all any of us can do.

The fear of further suicides in your family is less common than the experience of fleeting thoughts of dying yourself or the worry someone else in your family will die from other causes. I remember worrying a lot about my daughter. I was not concerned she would hurt herself, but I did worry she might get hit by a car. One loss tends to make the survivor worry about subsequent deaths. This anxiety does not last forever.

Many suicide survivors report this phenomenon during the first year or so.

STAYING IN ANGER OR GRIEF

I have not observed survivors who hold on to their grief or stay angry about the death for an extended period of time—more than 2 or 3 years. I do recognize that this is possible. I presume that the source of the extended grief is a desire to hold on to the loved one. When grief subsides, there is a certain distancing that occurs. One can almost say that there is grief that the grief is going.

In some cultures, one is taught that it is the duty of the bereaved to avenge the death of the loved one. Not being angry would imply that the deceased did not mean as much to the survivor as he or she should have. I wonder if sustained anger is not a means of affirming within oneself, while communicating to others, that the deceased was important and his death continues to affect the life of the survivor?

I will not criticize anyone who continues to grieve for many years or continues to be angry. It is not up to me to tell someone what they should do or how they should feel. I am just grateful that I have been blessed by being one of the lucky ones whose grief and anger subsided when it did.

If you are lucky, there are some effects from this death (from any major loss) which can produce personal growth.

LACK OF FEAR

One of the worst things that can happen to anyone has already happened to you. What terrible thing in the future could be more difficult to cope with than what you have already managed to survive? There is a measure of fearlessness which develops over time after the death.

Immediately following the suicide, there is usually an initial period when fear is heightened. You may fear another child will die accidentally or by suicide, that your spouse will die, or a friend of the suicide victim will also kill himself. After a year or so the fear subsides, and a calm realization descends. You have lived through this and come to realize you can withstand almost anything. You do not want further tragedies. You have had quite enough suffering for one lifetime. Your ordeal is as substantial as anything anyone has had to endure. Yet, you have chosen life and have survived.

GETTING PRIORITIES IN ORDER

There is nothing less inspiring than superficial values: the way your hair looks, the way your clothes fit, how much money you have, what car you drive, where your children went to college, etc. etc. etc. A suicide (or any great loss) is an effective means of coming to grips with what is really important. I used to have many hopes and dreams for my daughter. Now I only want her to continue to breathe from day to day. Her continuing to live is a priority for me. I have no control over it, but I do hope it will happen. I have hope, and the initial fear about her safety is gone.

WISDOM

A life lived with honesty and integrity will produce a measure of wisdom in mid-life and much wisdom in old age. Tragedy, honestly faced, also does this. I am constantly amazed by the wisdom of the members in our grief support group. I feel privileged to attend those meetings. Even if it were not my assigned duty to bring the box housing the little memorial library we began, it is likely I would come anyway. I meet some of the nicest and wisest people there.

A MEANING TO LIFE

Man's Search For Meaning is the story of Viktor Frankl's experience in Hitler's concentration camps. He and one sister were the only members of his family still alive after World War II. His ordeal taught him, "to live is to suffer, to survive is to find meaning in the suffering" (Frankl, X).

Tragedy is an integral part of life. If life has a purpose, then suffering has a purpose. Each person needs to discover for himself the meaning of painful tragedies and then act with responsibility to live out the purpose which underlies the suffering. Doing this brings nobility to the life of the survivor.

Some of Frankl's fellow prisoners died quickly in camp. The ones who survived were those who had what he called "a will to meaning." Prison is an opportunity to look inward, to grow. Suffering of any kind is a call to explore your deepest nature as a human being, to find inner beauty and spiritual freedom.

During the years of his confinement, Frankl had no way of knowing whether or not his wife was alive. One day he had a revelation. He came to understand that love goes beyond the physical body of the person you love. Its "deepest meaning is the spiritual being, the inner self." Whether or not the person is alive or not ultimately stops being important. The love exists independent of the physical existence of the beloved.

Ultimately, we have the freedom to choose what we shall do with our suffering. We can retain dignity even in the worst of circumstances. It is spiritual freedom, something no one can take from us, which gives life meaning and purpose. To achieve something from our suffering requires a belief that one's life is important and everyone's life is valuable. Each person's life is, in fact, a sacred story. When life is sacred, tragedies take on the significance of being the greatest test of our lives. Sacredness also implies that the suffering we endure has value for our future. This looking forward is an important ingredient in our awareness that life still expects something from us. The suffering we endure prepares us for the future in which we can choose to act to fulfill our fate.

It is everyone's destiny to suffer, for without it, life is incomplete. The value that comes from suffering is summarized by Frankl when he quoted Nietzsche—"that which does not kill me makes me stronger."

Advice From Other
Survivors

I never cease to be impressed by the wisdom of the people who regularly attend our suicide survivors' support group. I wanted to include them in the writing of this book. After completing the first draft of this manuscript, I wrote the following letter to the members of our group whose experience of loss was at least one year in length.

Hi.

One of the most helpful things for me during my bereavement has been writing. I am in the process of putting down some thoughts about my experience for the purpose of publication. I would appreciate it if you would be willing to share a little of your experience with me in the hope of helping others, should this manuscript ever become available to other suicide survivors.

The four topics I'd like to explore with you are:

1.   *The stages or cyclical nature of the grief process.*

In <u>The Gift of Hope</u>, Robert Veninga writes that people often function with energy right after a tragedy, but the period from 4 - 8 months after the death can be extremely painful. Personally I had fairly good spirits and high energy for two-and-a-half months after the death, followed by low energy and extremely low mood in the next four months. I then went through a period in which I was able to function fairly well each day as long as I had an opportunity to grieve and cry each day for 15 - 30 minutes. Within that time, however, I also experienced some days or weeks in which the grief was as intense as it had been during the worst months. This period lasted most intensely until approximately 14 months after Ben's death.   From then until now, I would say there has been a continuation of this type of pattern but in a less painful, raw form. (I still need to cry, but not daily. I still have painful times, but they are less frequent.)

What was your experience?

2.   *Things you found helpful during the bereavement.*

I obviously found reading, writing, and the support group the most helpful.   I also found renewed, intense relationships with my sisters and brothers to be very comforting. Conversations with one special friend with whom I could be totally honest have been a constant source of support.

What was your experience?

3.   *Other things you would particularly like to tell others about your grief experience.*

For example, in my relationships with other friends I have been hurt by the lack of courage of some who could not bring themselves to contact me more frequently during the bereavement.

Conversely, I was frankly amazed by the courage of a few people who did talk to me about painful subjects, knowing full well they would then have to deal with the pain of my grief. For those who do not know what to say I'd like to suggest sending a "thinking of you" card periodically or writing a very short letter as a way of communicating to the person that they are remembered with love. Friends are understandably hesitant about doing the wrong thing during a delicate or especially painful time following the death.

What have been the most helpful and/or the most hurtful experiences you have had with friends and family?

4.   *What things would you most like to communicate about your own personal experience?*

If you are willing to share some of your experiences, write down your thoughts on these topics and send them to me. If you are not interested in doing this, I want you to know I respect that decision.

Thanks!

Trudy

Three of our members generously shared their grief experience. Their writing moved me deeply and led me to write the following.

Dear Margaret, Monica, and Linda:

Thank you for writing about your experience after your son's death. When I originally planned on including your advice to other survivors in my manuscript, I thought of integrating your comments into several of the chapters I had written. But after reading your wonderful responses, I decided they were an entity unto themselves and should be left intact. I have now decided to put them together as a single chapter.

Your work offers sound advice to anyone reading the manuscript, as well as inspiration on how they too can write about their experience.

The format may be a helpful vehicle for other survivors to use.

I also would like to include a little biographical material on both you and your sons. It can be anything you choose. For example, you could say a little about yourself, the age your son died, the year he died, and a little about him.

Whatever you decide, I will respect your decision.

Sincerely,

Trudy

My fellow survivors were hesitant to write about themselves. This prompted me to write this follow-up letter.

Dear Monica:

Thank you for the very moving letter with its permission to use what you have written. I have one question. What do you want to say about yourself? I would like to include some information about your volunteer work with scouts, and any other work with children. I think it is about time it is made clear that these tragedies happen to good parents like yourself who spent a lot of time and energy helping not only their own children, but caring for and about other children in their community.

Your,

Trudy

Even with this encouragement, some of the fellow survivors were finding it difficult to write positive things about themselves. Their natural modesty made them hesitant to write some of the things other people can see so clearly.

Consequently, although the insights on survival are the writing of these generous and courageous women, the introductory material on Margaret and Monica was written by me.

MARGARET

Margaret is a well respected teacher who generously gives her time by participating in a number of educational task forces in her district. Her son Ross was an especially bright student whose aptitude tests placed him in the "gifted" category. He was well liked by fellow students and was active in sports.

In the months preceding his death, Ross became painfully thin. Concerned about his health, Margarget took him to their family physician who did not detect any physical problem. He tried to reassure her by saying that all of her children had been thin. He assumed Ross was just going through a teen growth spurt and his weight would ultimately catch up to the increased inches he had grown.

Ross shot himself on January 3, 1988 at the age of 13. He left an audio tape as a message to his family. It explained that he loved his family very deeply. His death was not in anyway anyone's fault. His decision to take his life had nothing to do with the outer circumstances of his life. It was just that all through his life he felt he just did not belong.

Margaret began attending the support group within weeks after her son's death. She very much wanted to grief his death in a way that would be positive for her and potentially helpful to others. After attending the group as a participant for two years, she received training through the grief center and served as one of the facilitators for the suicide support group for four years. It was during those six years she learned about the symptoms of depression and began to recognize Ross as displaying some of the signs during his childhood. Ross had been more irritable, never quite as relaxed and content with life as the her other children were as youngsters. Margaret also saw that in the months before his death, Ross began to withdrawn from his friends. These are subtle signs of depression that she hopes will become more commonly recognized as symptoms of an illness that is tragically painful for so many of our young people today.

Margaret's Response

Thank you, Trudy, for an opportunity to put my thoughts into writing. Five years have passed since the death of my youngest child. It would appear to most people that I am "healed." I look happy, laugh with friends, love my job and enjoy my other children. But, in reality, the pain of Ross's death is still there. It is different because now I feel such sadness because I did not know he was depressed and hurt so badly. I am so sorry I did not know so that I could have helped him. That is the pain -- the pain of regret. I think perhaps it will always be there.

The Stages Of Grief

The shock I felt when I discovered Ross's body lasted as a protection for eight months. I went through all the motions of living, but felt nothing, lacked energy, and lost all interest in the world around me except for the well-being of my two surviving children. After eight months, I felt the shock leave and with it, the cocoon that had been my insulation from the pain of Ross's death. Along with the pain came the beginning of healing, because then I could really begin to concentrate on reading and understanding what had caused this tragedy to occur.

The one phase of grief that eluded me was anger. I felt none: not toward Ross, God, or anyone else. I'm thankful for that because it allowed me to feel just regret - regret for all the things that would never be.

When two years had passed since Ross's death, I could feel acceptance of what had happened. I knew we would be okay and life would go on. It would never be the same; there would always be that empty place where Ross's life should have been, but there was hope.

Help During Bereavement

I knew immediately that our family would not survive in isolation. We surrounded ourselves with people who loved us and would listen to us talk about what had happened.

I joined the Suicide Survivors Group through our local grief support center just two weeks after Ross's death. I met with the director of the Grief Center, Ben Wolff, on a weekly basis for six months. I read everything I could find on suicide and depression. I wanted to grieve Ross's death in the healthiest way possible, and I knew that would only happen by talking about it with people who cared.

One dear friend called me every day for two years just to check on me. That was wonderful!

Relationships

My relationship with my other children became much stronger because we had shared such a traumatic experience. We lived it, discussed it, and grieved it together.

Two good friends were lost. They could not face me after the death; it hurt them too much. They did not know what to say and chose to stay away.

The people who still call or write mean so much to me. They remember Ross and talk about my precious child. I love them for that.

I would like to advise other survivors to:

1.   *talk about the loved one who died*

2.   *talk about the death*

3.   *talk about your feelings*

4.   *be selective with whom you share time; be with people who really care*

5.   *help others; speak when asked, meet one-to-one with other survivors*

6.   *read everything you can about suicide and depression*

7. *join a support group where you live to be with people who understand*

8.   *get counseling to help you*

9. *know that acceptance will come and with it healing and hope for the future*

10.   *be a resource for others*

MONICA

Monica is a homemaker who worked as a substitute teacher's aid at our local elementary school. She was active in many programs that benefit children, including scouts. Although she and her husband were very concerned about their son Jery's learning problems (an attention deficit hyperactive disorder), this condition was never fully diagnosed.

Jery was well liked by his peers. His great sense of humor was probably his way of coping with the pain caused by his learning disability and depression. On September 4, 1990, Jerry shot himself at the age of 15. His death came as a complete surprise to his loving family who had not seen any signs of depression in the son who was such a joy to them.

Both Monica and her husband began attending the suicide support group soon after Jery's death. At first, all they were being told about the signs of depression did not seem to apply to their son. Jery seemed so happy and was so much fun to have around that it did not make sense that someone like him could have been suffering from a mood disorder. Only gradually were they were able to relate Jery's inability to sleep as an important clue that something was wrong.

Monica's Response

The Stages Of Grief

Shock carried me through the first couple of months after my son Jery's death. After that, it has been a rough roller coaster of emotions. It started violently and is now more expected less overwhelming. Adjustment to grief is the hardest process I have ever experienced. Daily functioning is still a real chore at times. Time itself is hard to keep track of. But as I have read and heard others say, the extreme pain does subside as time goes on.

Help During Grief

The things that have been most helpful to me are: faith in God to make all things right, the support of my church, my husband's support and constant attention, and conversations with others who have also had the tragic loss of a child. I have had the good fortune of being able to learn from people who understand the grief process. I have sometimes felt alone during my grief, but when I talk with others who understand grief, they make me feel less alone.

Things I would like to tell others about grief

Grief work is very taxing. I got physically exhausted from it at times. I found myself experiencing waves of pain. I questioned everything I believed in. It is difficult to control the strong anger I had never felt before in my life and to attempt to accept the unacceptable. I found the ignorance of friends and family hurtful and the compassion and understanding of others comforting.

What I would most like to communicate about my personal experience

After my son's death, I lost all confidence in myself. My son's death made me feel as if I had failed the test of my life. I was also afraid to get close to anyone because I never wanted to feel such pain again. Day by day I struggle to be of some use to myself and others. I struggle to give life some kind of meaning.

I feel so blessed to have had Jery in my life. He was many different things to many different people. My memories of him haunted me at first. Now they comfort me. I look forward to seeing him when the time comes. Until then, I will keep a warm glow in my heart each time I think of him.

Knowing there is no correct way to grieve gave me the freedom to heal in my own way and in my own time.   My husband grieves in his own way and we respect each others way of dealing with the pain. We encourage each other to go on with life and find what comfort and joy we can in it.

Yes, the loss of a dearly loved one is life changing. What we would not give to not go through this, but what a gift to survive and keep on learning.

LINDA

Bobby was our oldest child; we have another son and a daughter. He died on December 26, 1986, as a result of suicide. It is still hard to believe, even as I write this, seven years later. We have always been a very close family and our children came first, but I still feel guilty. Somehow I must have failed as a mother.

Bobby had some problems prior to his death. He was studying to become a surgical technician and had failed one of his classes. Consequently, he needed to wait until the next fall to go back to school. A very good friend of our son committed suicide the previous April, and I know this was very hard on everyone. Ironically, I was involved in telling the friend's mother about her son's death and six months later it was our nightmare as well. Bobby had been dating his girlfriend for a year and a half, and they broke up before his death. I think these three things were just more than Bobby could handle.

Bobby was a medic in the Army National Guard which was something he was very proud of. He was a very good water skier and both he and his brother had mastered the art of barefoot skiing. Bobby had a great sense of humor and loved pulling pranks on all of us. His favorite movies and television shows were all comedies.

Bobby was handsome, with beautiful blue eyes and long eyelashes. From the time he was a baby, people always commented on his pretty eyes, but he never seemed to realize just how good looking he was.

It is hard to see Bobby's friends getting married and having children. The weddings are more difficult than funerals; Bobby had a funeral but he did not have a wedding or children.

Our family has a lot of compassion for others who are grieving a loss. I have learned to accept the fact that Bobby is gone. There will always be an empty space in my heart and our family, but life goes on. I know Bobby is at peace and must have had so much emotional pain that he could not go on. Someone told me, "Our children are not supposed to die before us, it is a death out of turn. When you bury your parents your bury your past, but when you bury your children, you bury your future." It is so true. My mother died from cancer a year before

Bobby's death. I was sitting with her when she died and had time to tell her how much I loved her. When Bobby died we did not have a chance to tell him good-bye, and we were not allowed to see him after he died. His death was so sudden and so final. I know we will be together again someday and am very thankful we had him for those 20 years. I am also thankful for my husband, our other children, our granddaughters, and other members of our family. Bobby would want all of us to be happy.

Linda's Response

Stages

I enjoy doing crafts projects, but I just could not do any for at least six months. I did not have the interest or the energy for crafts. I wept every day for a year. Some of the worst times were when I was driving in the car by myself and would hear a song that reminded me of Bobby. Television shows about someone with a broken heart are still painful for me. Sometimes I still cry when I am alone. I am afraid one day I will not be able to stop crying and will go crazy. I am still very afraid something might happen to my other two children or my granddaughters. I do not think I could keep my sanity if I lost one of them. I probably smother my daughter, Jodie. We are overly protective of her but she understands. She is very thoughtful, and both of our children are very compassionate.

Bobby died in December of 1986, the day after Christmas. Naturally, the holidays are hard for us, and I have a hard time sharing my children with other people during the holidays. I want them to be with us. I am adjusting to this, and the grandchildren have made our holidays much more bearable. I know I am much stronger than I ever thought I was. I am going to survive this trauma.

What Helps

I started reading books for entertainment. I did not read much before Bobby died. Now I read at night when I cannot sleep. The suicide survivors support group was a life saver.

It was helpful for me to participate on panels at two suicide seminars with several other mothers. I felt good doing this, and I think we helped other people to understand. It gave us an opportunity to tell others that suicide can happen in a good family.

I have two very good friends who started taking walks with me every morning at 8:00. This gave me a reason to get up each morning. I feel I could talk to them anytime. They are terrific. I was surprised when some of the people who I would have expected to be there for me were not. Some of my friends avoided me. My sister, Nancy, was Bobby's godmother. We have always been very close. She is great.

What I particularly want to communicate

In the beginning, I felt guilty if I laughed or had an especially good time. But I know Bobby would want us all to be happy. I know he really loved us, and we were always there for him.

I really appreciate anyone who mentions Bobby. It is nice to know other people have not forgotten him. It has been nice to receive a card on his birthday or occasionally just a "thinking of you" card.

CAROL

Early in 1994 the director of our grief center received a letter from a mother living on the east coast. She requested suggestions of books that would be helpful to suicide survivors. Her letter was referred to me as the librarian of our support group. In the exchange of letters that followed, Carol indicated that she had thought of writing about her experience. I sent her a copy of the format my friends had used to organize their thoughts. Here is what Carol wrote.

Carol's Response

My name is Carol and I was 41 when my 19 year old son committed suicide by hanging himself in his girlfriend's garage after an argument and breakup. I had three children by my first marriage: two daughters and my son. When my son was twelve my second husband and I adopted two more children: a girl and a boy.

We had no warning or indication, of any kind, that a suicide could happen. Two months before the death, our family moved from Florida to Virginia. Our son had decided to stay in Florida with his girlfriend. I spoke to him the day before he killed himself. He seemed in very good spirits and was planning a trip to Virginia to be with us for Christmas. Unfortunately, we brought him home for Christmas to bury him.

The stages of grief.

The first year and a half I had tremendous energy to research, read, write, and contact anyone connected with suicide. I studied all about suicide, took training classes in bereavement counseling, and reached out to other families as they too became survivors of tragedy. Then, suddenly and without warning, I took a serious nose-dive into deep depression. My health began to slowly deteriorate. I cried easily and often. I gave up on wanting to have a useful life. I did not care about housework, the younger children's school work, or myself.

When I hit the three year mark, I was severely depressed and found a death wish growing within me. I would sit and plan how I could die without having it look like a suicide, so that my family would not feel guilty. Then one day (two months after the three year mark) I checked out yet another book on suicide from our local library. The book contained a list of suicide survivors groups. I decided to write to them to see if I really was going crazy or if this depressed mood was just part of the grief process.

I was overwhelmed at the response. The number one suggestion I received was to get help fast. Finding a suicide survivors support group in my area, as well as seeking individual professional help would be very helpful to me. Unfortunately, I could not find a suicide survivors group in my city, but did find a Christian Counseling Center. I made an appointment with a grief counselor and began receiving some help.

I finally feel I am coming out of the long dark tunnel I have been in for so long. I am working very hard on doing my grief work. I need to let go of my guilt, accept the fact that my son is gone, and learn to forgive myself for all I did or did not do in his lifetime.

Things that were helpful during bereavement.

Reading, reading, reading. Finding someone to talk to about my son was also very helpful, but unfortunately, I did not have an opportunity to do so very often. Being able to say his name without someone changing the subject helped me. When I would get letters from people expressing their sympathy, it really helped because I felt they were acknowledging my pain.

Writing was also an excellent outlet. I did not realize it at the time, but writing probably helped save my sanity. Since I had recently moved to a new part of the country just two months before my son's death, I had not had time to make any close friends or develop strong relationships with a church. I felt very alone. Without the support of family and friends, writing allowed me to express my pain. Screaming on paper served to release my shock and disbelief.

The most helpful thing of all was when other parents, especially mothers of sons who also committed suicide, called me or came to see me. I needed to ask them a million questions about what I was going through.   Their willingness to periodically check in on me served as a lifeline for me.

Other things I would like to share about my personal grief experience.

I soon learned that some of the people I considered my friends turned the other way, as if there was some dread disease in my family that could be contagious. Even my own family treated my son's suicide as a disgrace and would not come to the funeral. I do not understand why my old neighbors, whose children grew up with my son, attending school with him from kindergarten to high school, did not get in touch with me. They did not send cards, flowers, or even call me. This hurt the most.

The other thing that hurt me greatly were the well-meaning people who said things like: "When are you going to get over this?" (It was only three months since the death.) "Well, he chose to do this, so just let him go!" (As if he felt he had any choices left.) "It was God's will." (What kind of a God do they have? My God loves me too much to hurt me like this!) And the very worst comment anyone ever makes to a parent of a child who has committed suicide. "Well, you realize your son's soul went to hell because suicide is an unforgivable sin in the eyes of the church." (I want to scream at that one! There is nothing in scripture or from any reputable clergy that supports such an ignorant statement.)

Things I would like to communicate about my own experience.

As bad as it seems at any given point, you have already survived the WORST POSSIBLE DAY OF YOUR LIFE—the day your child died. You survived that day and although it seems unbearable, you can survive every day from then on. Time does not heal all wounds, but it does help ease the intensity of the pain you have to bear. Hold on. It really is always darkest before the dawn.

Conclusion

O h my God, Ben is dead! The news of my son's suicide would hit my consciousness with fresh awareness each morning during those first months after his death. I can't tell you when I awoke and thought of something else first - "Let's see, today is a work day, it is Tuesday, it's snowy; better wear my boots, I have these appointments, I'll have to remember to do such and such. Ben is dead." Only someone who has been through a grief process like ours knows we rediscover the suicide each morning.

This book was intended for the newly bereaved, to help them through the first two or three years, the most painful part of their grief work. It was also intended for their family and friends, many of whom genuinely want to understand but have no way of knowing what helps unless they are told. Most of them want to be helpful, but they struggle to find a way. Perhaps you'll want to pass this book on to them, or tell them where to get it.

No one can take away your pain. I do not believe it would be good for you even if it were possible. Ultimately, wisdom can come from all this suffering. You have been robbed of your loved one. Should you also be robbed as well of the potential growth that can come from such a profound experience? Although you can't avoid the necessary pain of your grief, you have the right to be spared unnecessary pain. Five months after Ben's death, I attended a weekend workshop for bereaved parents. One speaker described what had been done at the hospital to heighten the awareness of the staff and/or visitors to the facility in cases where the mother had lost her baby. Maternity wards are usually the happiest unit in any hospital. To avoid having someone bound into the bereaved mother's room and cheerfully ask her a totally innocent question like, "Was your baby a boy or a girl?", the staff put a picture of a broken heart outside the door. This communicated to everyone that hers is not a happy room. It saved everyone unnecessary pain because the person asking the question suffers right along with the mother when they innocently ask questions requiring painful answers.

I know of no way suicide survivors can wear a sign around their neck saying, "Do not ask me how many children I have" (when the suicide victim was their child), or "Do not ask me how many brothers or sisters I have" (when the person who killed himself was a sibling), or "Do not ask me what my husband does?" (when the person who died was your spouse). I can't begin to imagine what a child says when someone asks him about his mother if she died by suicide. All of these benign questions strangers ask may be part of the unavoidable pain survivors experience. All that is possible is to pass on tips to those who do know what has happened to help them learn how to be helpful rather than hurtful.

What do you say to a suicide survivor? I recall one evening when my daughter and her friend were over to our house for dinner. One of Caroline's school friends had recently taken his life. I told her I did not have any idea what to say to the bereaved mother. Even though I had taught psychology at the university level and my own son had died just a few years earlier, I felt I was in the same position as everyone else is when confronting a new suicide survivor - What do you say?

I have a niece who lost her four year old daughter following a surgery. When she sent me a sympathy card at the time of Ben's death she wrote "There are no words." The wisdom of my young niece's remarks is that friends who listen intently and speak little are more helpful than friends who talk a lot and listen little.

I too wish to be a careful listener. If in the months or years ahead your grief work teaches you something I have not included in these pages concerning how to deal with guilt or anger, please let me know. If you discover other ways of dealing with others or things that got you through painful times or special occasions, pass your suggestions to me. I hope this book has been useful in its present form. It will likely be even more useful when it is revised some day to include some new material coming from you and from research which may yet reveal further answers to the most pressing question: Why?

Works Cited

Campbell, J. (1990). <u>Transformations of myth through time</u>.
New York: Harper & Row.

Fawcett, J.A., M.D. (1992). Short- and long-term predictors of
suicide in depressed patients. <u>Lifesavers: The Newsletter of
the American Suicide Foundation</u>.

Fieve, F.R., M.D. (1975). <u>Moodswings</u>. New York: Bantam
Books.

Fishman, K.D. (1991, June). Therapy for children. <u>The Atlantic
Monthly</u>, pp. 47-69.

Frankl, V.E. (1959). <u>Man's search for meaning</u>. New York:
Washington Square Press.

Gold, M.S. (1987). <u>The good news about depression</u>. New
York: Bantam Books.

Goode, E. (1990, March 5). Beating depression. <u>U.S. News &
World Report</u>, pp. 48-55.

Mental Health Advocate. (1991, Aug.-Sept.).

Popper, C., M.D. (1989). Diagnosing bipolar vs. ADHD, American Academy of Child and Adolescent Psychiatry News. Washington DC

Roy, A., (1992). Schizophrenia and suicide. Lifesavers: The Newsletter of the American Suicide Foundation.

Sargent, M. (a). Depressive illnesses: Treatment brings new hope. U.S. Department of Health and Human Services. National Institute of Mental Health.

Sheehan, D.V. (1983). The anxiety disease. New York: Bantam Books.

Useful information on suicide. (1986). U.S. Department of Health and Human Services. National Institute of Mental Health.

Veninga, R.L. (1985). A gift of hope: How we survive our tragedies. New York: Ballantine Books.

Weissman, M., Ph.D. (1991). Panic and suicidal behavior. Lifesavers: The Newsletter of the American Suicide Foundation.

What is depression. Mental Health Association of Greater Duluth.

Further References

Adolescent stress and depression. (1986). Teens in distress. University of Minnesota: Minnesota Extension Service.

Beck, Rush, Shaw, and Emery (1979). Cognitive Therapy of Depression. New York: Guilford Press.

Burns, D.D., M.D. (1980). Feeling good: The new mood therapy. New York: Signet Books.

Gorman, M.D. (1990). The Essential Guide to Psychiatric Drugs. New York: St. Martin's Press.

Elmer-Dewitt, P. (1992, July 6). Depression: The growing role of drug therapies. Time, pp. 57-59.

Hewett, J.H. (1980). After suicide. Philadelphia, Pennsylvania: The Westminster Press.

Hoberman, H.M., Ph.D. (1989). Completed suicide in children and adolescents: A review. In B.D. Garfinkel (Ed.), Adolescent suicide: Recognition, treatment, and prevention. New York: Haworth.

Klerman, G., Weissman, M., Rounsaville, B., & Chevron, E.
(1984). <u>Interpersonal psychotherapy of depression</u>. New
York: Basic Books, Inc.

Kubler-Ross, Elisabeth. (   ). <u>Death, the final growth stage</u>.

Larson, D.E., M.D. (Ed.). (1990). <u>Mayo Clinic family health
book.</u> New York: William Morrow and Company, Inc.

McKay, M. & Fanning, P. (1987). <u>Self esteem</u>. Oakland,
California: New Harbinger Publications.

McKnew, D.H., Cytryn, L., & Yahraes, H. (1983). <u>Why isn't
Johnny crying? Coping with depression in children</u>. New
York: Norton & Company.

Papolos, D., and Papolos, J. (1992). <u>Overcoming depression</u>.
New York: Harper Perennial.

Sargent, M. (b). Helping the depressed person get treatment.
U.S. Department of Health and Human Services. <u>National
Institute of Mental Health.</u>

Sarnoff Schiff, H. (1977). The bereaved parent. New York: Penguin Books.

Supporting distressed young people. (1985). Teens in distress. University of Minnesota: Minnesota Extension Service.

Supporting young people following a suicide. (1986) Teens in distress. University of Minnesota: Minnesota Extension Service.

Teen suicide. (1985). Teens in distress. University of Minnesota: Minnesota Extension Service.

Understanding the new risk factors for suicide. (1991, Summer). Lifesavers: The Newsletter of the American Suicide Foundation.

Wrobleski, A. (1991). Suicide survivors: A guide for those left behind. Minneapolis, Minnesota: Afterwords Publishing.

Index

ABOUT THE AUTHOR

Trudy Carlson never intended to write this book. One year before the death of her son she was inspired to write a manuscript dealing with her life-long interest: the psychological interpretation of famous stories. Ben's death changed everything. She temporarily put the first book aside to begin writing the story of his life. She needed to record everything about the problems she observed during the various stages of his life, all the things she did to help him and the attempt to obtain treatment for his condition. The effect his life and death had on her became the focus of her writing.

As she worked she discovered she had three separate topics. The first became <u>The Suicide of My Son: A Story of Childhood Depression</u>. It focuses on the little understood symptoms of depressive illness and anxiety disorders in youngsters. Using her son's life as an example of these conditions, the manuscript takes a no-fault approach to explaining the biological nature of these conditions. It describes how a school-based program can be an inexpensive and effective way of treating students twelve years of age and older.

<u>Learning Disabilities: A Guide to Recognizing and Managing Learning and Behavioral Problems in Children,</u>

contrasts Ben's difficulty with ADHD (Attentional Deficit Hyperactive Disorder) with her own personal struggle with a mild case of dyslexia. The contrast between her success in overcoming her disability is explained in terms of the differences in the nature of the two learning problems, the particular way each condition affects the life of the person, the type of school environment each experienced, and the sheer number of problems Ben faced. Generic no cost/low cost programs helpful for a wide range of difficulties faced by elementary aged youngsters today are described.

Tragedy, Finding a Hidden Meaning: How to Transform the Tragedies in Your Life into Personal Growth, explores the personal and spiritual growth that can emerge from loss. The manuscript uses the wisdom found in enduring stories (fairy tales, stories from the lives of others who overcame difficult circumstances, and stories found in the major religions throughout the world) to demonstrate a way to discover a personal meaning in an otherwise seemingly meaningless tragedy. Carl Jung wrote, "Meaning makes most things endurable, perhaps everything." This book demonstrates how Ms. Carlson discovered meaning in her son's life and his death. Other books on bereavement focus on the process of recovery. This manuscript shows how a search for meaning can reduce unnecessary suffering. It may be helpful to anyone experiencing a loss of any kind.

While working on revisions of these manuscripts, she realized she needed to write a book of practical advice for fellow survivors. It became this book, Suicide Survivors Handbook: A Guide for the Bereaved and Those Who Wish to Help Them.

ORDER FORM

Telephone orders: Call Toll Free: 1-800-296-7163
Have your Visa or MasterCard number ready
Postal Orders: Benline Press, P.O. Box 3032
        Mt. Royal Station, Duluth, MN. 55803.

Please send the following books. I understand that I may return
any books for a full refund -- for any reason, no questions asked.

Suicide Survivor's Handbook: A Guide to the Bereaved and
Those Who Wish to Help Them $14.95 _____

The Suicide of My Son: A Story of Childhood Depression
                                        $16.95 _____

Forthcoming Books

Tragedy, Finding a Hidden Meaning: How to Transform
the Tragedies in Your Life into Personal Growth   _____

Learning Disabilities: How to Recognize and Manage,
Learning and Behavioral Problems in Children   _____

Sales Tax: Please add 7.5% for books shipped to Minnesota
addreses   _____
Shipping: Book Rate: $2.00 for the first book and 75 cents for
each additonal book (Surface shipping may take three
to four weeks)   Airmail: $3.50 per book
                                        Total   _____

Payment: __ check __ credit card
Card Number:_____
Name on card:_____Exp. Date _____/_____